Excellent at the Beginning

Excellent at the Beginning

Discovering the Buddhist Way

By Khenpo Karthar Rinpoche

Translated by Chöjor Radha

Additional translations by
Karma Yeshe Gyamtso and Ngödup Burkhar

RINCHEN PUBLICATIONS
KINGSTON, NEW YORK, USA

Published by:
Rinchen, Inc.
20 John Street
Kingston, NY 12401
(845) 331-5069
www.rinchen.com

First Edition; September, 2015

ISBN: 978-0-9714554-4-3

This book is dedicated to
His Holiness Ogyen Trinley Dorje,
the Seventeenth Gyalwang Karmapa

IN MEMORY OF

Chöjor Radha

1954-2009

CONTENTS

Introduction

There is a saying in the Buddhist tradition that what the Buddha taught is "excellent at the beginning, excellent in the middle, and excellent at the end." What this means is that his teachings are wonderful and valuable when we first encounter them, and continue to be so all the way until we become enlightened. Another meaning in this saying is that the most basic teachings are truly extraordinary. They are especially so, because they can establish a correct foundation for our entire journey of the path.

This book is a collection of such wonderful and valuable introductory teachings. The material that makes it up was taught in live seminar settings by Khenpo Karthar Rinpoche in the Tibetan language, translated on the spot into English, and recorded. Since then, the teachings have been transcribed and carefully edited and reviewed. At the time of those seminars (from the mid-1980s through the early 1990s), there were many people who were completely new to Buddhism, and Rinpoche patiently and methodically gave many wonderful presentations of this basic material from his vast knowledge of the Tibetan tradition.

Of course, there are still many people who can benefit from a clear and genuine presentation of Buddhism, "from the beginning." If that is you, this book is going to be just right. But it is also true that if you have been around a while with Buddhism it is great to review the teachings and get new perspectives on familiar topics. Therefore, I can also say that more experienced students will get a lot out of it too.

When I think of someone encountering the authentic Buddhist teachings through this book, I feel real happiness. May it bring joy and blessings to all who read it! By joining your study and contemplation with diligence in practice, may your journey bring inspiration, wellbeing, and genuine awakening.

Acknowledgements

To truly give credit where it is due for this book, we must begin by honoring His Holiness Rangjung Rigpe Dorje, the 16th Gyalwang Karmapa, who established Karma Triyana Dharmachakra (KTD) in Woodstock New York in the 1970s, and who sent Ven. Khenpo Karthar Rinpoche to the United States to be KTD's Abbott and main teacher.

What an incredible kindness it was of the 16th Karmapa to send us such a teacher! Since 1976, Khenpo Karthar Rinpoche has guided and inspired thousands of students with his great kindness and wisdom, and through his example of purity and energy in benefiting everyone he encounters. He is now over 90 years old and is continuing to teach and lead us with amazing strength. This book is but a drop of the vast ocean of his teaching activity in the nearly 40 years he has lived in America.

The successor of the 16th Karmapa, His Holiness the Seventeenth Karmapa Ogyen Trinley Dorje, to whom this book is dedicated, is now 30 years old, and has visited KTD three times. He is a dynamic and vastly inspiring teacher and leader. Very much a man of the 21st Century, he is dedicated to the environment, human rights, and to moving the ancient tradition he represents decisively into the future. May everyone who encounters this book make a connection with His Holiness the 17th Karmapa.

It is with gratitude and remembrance that we honor the work of the late Chöjor Radha, who translated all but two of the sections of this book. Chöjor was a truly lovable, dear person, someone whose very being was infused with the good qualities of Buddhist practice. He always brought a lot of humor and wit to his job while translating for the lamas. Chöjor was medically frail due to tragic circumstances that he suffered as a Tibetan refugee, and which led to his premature death in 2009. Despite his health challenges, he never complained. He also never took himself too seriously despite being from a very prominent Tibetan family (his uncle was the famous Dilgo Khentse Rinpoche, and his brother is Chime Rinpoche, a highly regarded lama who lives in England.) We in the KTD community loved Chöjor dearly, and truly miss him. I hope this book and the blessings it will bring are a fitting testament to his lifelong service to Buddhism.

My thanks also go to Lama Kathy Wesley of Columbus Karma Thegsum Choling (an affiliate center of KTD) for her long support of this collection of teachings. In large part through her leadership, this material has been used in transcript form with great benefit at KTD and its local centers for quite some time.

Naomi Schmidt did a wonderful job of typesetting the book, and she showed a lot of patience in the face of the delays that came up in its completion. Naomi was also editor of KTD's Densal Magazine—where many of these teachings originally appeared—for a span of 27 years (1982-2009). I honor her for her many decades of service to the Buddhist community.

The original compilation of this material into one integrated anthology was done at Heart Center KTC, under the direction and sponsorship of Michael and Margaret Erlewine. It is but a small part of the prodigious work they have done over many years in support of their teacher and the KTD community. Robert Walker served as editor in this first phase of publication, clarifying many points with the translators, and with Rinpoche as needed.

When Rinchen Publications took up the publication in book form, Florence Wetzel did a tremendous amount of excellent editorial work. I would also like to thank Drolma Birney for her fine editing of the last chapter of the book, which was an addition to the original anthology. When editing was complete, the whole manuscript was skillfully proofread by Arya-francesca Jenkins and Sharon Philbrook.

Especially when you see the rather large number of other community members listed in the credits at the very end of the book, you will conclude that this truly was a community project, spanning quite a long period of time. I thank everyone who made a contribution, and feel honored to have served as managing editor and publisher. As such, I take full responsibility for any errors or shortcomings in expressing the clarity of Rinpoche's teachings.

David McCarthy
President, Rinchen Publications
July, 2015

Connecting with
the Buddhist Teachings

When we encounter the Buddhist teachings, it is entirely reasonable to question their purpose and benefit. How can we relate them to the present-day world and apply them in our own lives? And how might we connect with this tradition in a meaningful way?

The teachings of the Buddha are known as the Dharma, which is a Sanskrit word. The Tibetan word for the Dharma is *chö*, and it is interesting to note that the original meaning of *chö* in Tibetan is "correcting what is incorrect," "straightening what is bent," or "curing what is sick." In simplest terms, Dharma straightens us out. It is a remedy. The Buddha's teachings help us correct ourselves and the way we live our lives.

Buddhism has spread to many cultures and is now practiced by people in quite a few languages and with diverse customs. As a result, people sometimes wonder if it is just a set of Asian customs and beliefs, or if the form of Buddhism they encounter perhaps reflects the culture of a particular country more than the essential teachings of the Buddha.

In fact, that is not so. For example, the Buddhist teachings brought to the West by Tibetan masters are referred to as Tibetan Buddhism, yet the history of Buddhism goes back 2500 years to India. The teachings brought to Tibet from India are in fact the

1

same ones Tibetan masters give in the West. The term "Tibetan Buddhism" should refer to the fact that these teachings were brought here by Tibetans who were exiled from their country, but it should not mean that the Tibetans created them.

Since Buddhism came to Tibet over a thousand years ago, hundreds of thousands of people have studied, practiced, and become realized, freeing themselves from suffering, confusion, and dissatisfaction. Yet during that time, the culture and customs of Tibet and India have remained separate. When Buddhism is passed on by experienced teachers from an unbroken lineage, what is transmitted is the essence of the teachings, and this goes beyond any particular culture or custom.

A parallel can be drawn with the fact that different languages have different words for the same object. The English word fire, the Tibetan word *may*, and the French word *feu* all have the same meaning. The term which communicates the meaning is unimportant as long as we are all talking about the same thing. The thing referred to by the word, whether the word is fire, *feu*, or *may*, has the same effect: it burns. Despite the particular cultural way of using language, the essence of fire remains the same, and it is the same with the Dharma.

Before the communists invaded Tibet in 1959, the teachings were practiced by a large portion of the population. Those who left Tibet brought a vigorous, living tradition wherever they went. This tradition quickly took root in the West because it presented a direct opportunity for people to study and practice a living Dharma tradition. From this perspective, the communist invasion had a good effect. Since Buddhism was strong in Tibet, the destruction of Tibet had the effect of a big fire whose sparks spread all over the world, each one igniting a new flame. If Buddhism had degenerated before the communists came, then those who left would have had nothing to offer but ashes, which could not give birth to a new fire. Buddhism is therefore a living tradition which has come from India to Tibet, and now to the West.

An individual's involvement with the Dharma actually comes both from past causes and present circumstances. Past causes refer not only to this life, but to connections you had with the spiritual path in previous lives, particularly with Buddhism. There is no doubt that we were probably very well-connected with the Dharma in past lives, and that we are drawn to Buddhism in this life as a continuation of that habit. Because of this, we are interested in the study of Dharma and in virtuous actions generally. Without those past connections and habitual patterns, it would be impossible for us to have a strong desire to practice Dharma. It would be similar to giving grass to a meat-eating animal such as a tiger: the tiger would not be motivated to eat grass because tigers have the habit of eating meat. Similarly, motivation to practice Dharma comes from some past connection.

At the same time, the past connections we may have had with the Buddhist way are not sufficient in themselves. Present circumstances are also necessary. Spiritual friends, other Dharma practitioners, and a location where people practice meditation are essential conditions to awaken our past connection with the Dharma. This is similar to a seed that has the potential to grow and bear fruit, but cannot do so without the conditions of proper soil, moisture, and warmth.

All of us have enlightenment within ourselves, which is called the "buddha nature." However, meeting with the necessary causes and conditions is essential in order to actually *experience* the awakened state. For example, if you think back to the early history of the United States, Buddhism was not yet established. Although at that time everyone in this country had the potential for enlightenment, Buddhist centers, teachers, books, and so forth were not available. Therefore, even though people had the potential for enlightenment, they were unable to awaken it because they lacked the correct conditions. Nowadays people are fortunate because the necessary causes and conditions can be brought together. Many Western students have told me that although they had decent jobs, good families, and a number of different spiritual paths to choose from, they still felt that something was missing. Based on that feeling of incompleteness, they searched until they found Buddhism. This is what we mean by encountering the appropriate circumstances.

Returning to the example of the seed, even if a seed with the potential to grow meets with the right kind of soil, water, and warmth, that seed may not be able to grow if there is not a continual presence of warmth and moisture. Similarly, to awaken enlightened mind, it is not sufficient to meet with the right conditions just once; such possibilities must be available in a continuous way. That is why it was not sufficient for His Holiness the 16th Gyalwa Karmapa to visit and give teachings in the West once or twice. Seeing the importance of continuity in order to awaken the minds of each one of us, he established Karma Triyana Dharmachakra (KTD) monastery in Woodstock, New York. He also requested other teachers to visit KTD so that we could continue to cultivate our enlightened energy, and that by virtue of this continuity we could one day experience the fullness of enlightenment. Many other Buddhist teachers, in the Tibetan tradition as well as others, have established Dharma centers for the same reason.

If you are not familiar with these teachings, you may question whether such an old tradition is relevant to our present age. When the Buddha presented the Dharma, he based his words on personal experience and insight, particularly his realization that all beings experience suffering, pain, and dissatisfaction. The Dharma was beneficial in the past because it addressed this suffering, and it remains relevant today because it addresses the same problems. Therefore, these teachings are valuable no matter who you are, or when or where you live. It is like water and thirst: whether you lived thousands of years ago or are living now, water did and always will quench thirst.

Still, we might have questions about whether Buddhism is truly relevant to us. We might agree that in a remote place like Tibet, Buddhism must have been helpful in many ways, as well as useful to people who had few sources of entertainment. However, in our modern world with so much of everything, what else could we need?

The problem in today's world is that we are continually busy and restless. People in the past were never so busy; they did not live as we do, constantly engaged in a frustrating race against time. If we closely examine this constant push and nonstop restlessness, if we pay attention to why we live this way, we might acknowledge that we are caught up in this busyness because we want to experience greater harmony, satisfaction, and peace of mind.

Although we deeply desire psychological peace, the truth is that we are constantly making ourselves busy, which only brings us more dissatisfaction, frustration, and pain. Some things may bring temporary relief, but the very fact that the relief is temporary and thus uncertain also disturbs us. We have to face the suffering of both the pain we currently experience, and the pain that will come in the future when the relief passes. Looking further, we may realize that the way we run our lives could use some correction, some straightening out. If we could have just a tiny bit more control of our minds—control in the sense of knowing that we can count on the state of mind we are experiencing—that assurance could make an enormous difference in the quality of our lives.

What we need to experience, and what we can experience, is a saner, gentler state of mind. This experience is not found in something outside of ourselves. No material object can bring a calm, gentle state of mind. If we continually try to rely on external things as the way to experience fullness of mind and richness of heart, it will never work. Outside objects might give temporary relief, but we cannot afford to depend upon impermanent solutions. No one has succeeded with this approach in the past, and no one will in the future. If we think about this for a moment, this point is quite obvious. Our lives are too precious for that, too full of potential. We must work with our own minds and our own abilities in order to have rich, peaceful minds.

An example might help illustrate this point. Suppose someone is lying in bed and suffering from an ulcer. It is quite painful, so the person shifts from side to side, tries bigger or smaller pillows, and continuously changes things, seeking some degree of comfort. This relief is transitory, however, because the problem is an internal issue which is not due to external things such as the bed or pillows. Manipulating these external supports will not resolve the situation, but when the person receives proper internal medical treatment, he or she can be cured.

Similarly, we all have the potential to experience an abundant and harmonious mind, no matter how discouraged we may feel about ourselves, and no matter how impossible we think it might be to change our state of mind. It is also true that in order to be of better service to our world, we must persevere in training ourselves in the proper way. We need to cultivate a gentle, clear mind, free from confusion, a mind that does not distort our lives and potential and ceases to bring harm to ourselves and others.

This is why Buddhism emphasizes meditation—simple techniques that tame the mind. No matter how wild, uncomfortable, or confused your mind may be, there are methods of meditation that will tame it, and I would like to share these methods with you. Although I am in the declining years of my life, I hope to be around for a while longer. If you meditate, practicing properly and consistently, I can assure you that you will gradually experience a state of mind that will make a great difference in your life. I would like to be around to see you experience that!

Listening, Contemplating, and Meditating:

The Methods of Buddhist Practice

A s human beings, we all have the capacity to develop profound understanding, compassion, and wisdom. This is true whether you are male or female, rich or poor, or whatever your race, nationality, or background may be. This potential is naturally present in each of us, but we need a method in order to first recognize it, then understand it, and finally develop it fully.

According to the Buddhist tradition, those who have fully developed their inner potential are called "enlightened" beings, and those who have not are called "ordinary" or "sentient" beings. When we hear about the extraordinary qualities and abilities of enlightened beings, they may seem completely beyond us, and outside the realm of possibilities of our own experience. However, in terms of their *capacity*, enlightened beings actually do not have anything that we do not have. Although it may seem impossible, as ordinary beings we also have the same extraordinary abilities within ourselves. We just need to learn how to unfold that potential.

You might ask, "Since we have these enlightened qualities within ourselves, won't we just attain enlightenment naturally?" The answer is no. The process of unfolding our wisdom and the purification of our mental obscurations does not happen on its own, without effort or intention. The Buddhist view is that we have had countless lives throughout beginningless time, but we are still ordinary, unenlightened beings because we have not applied the methods needed to reveal our inherent wisdom. Likewise, regardless of how many lives we have in the future, we will remain unenlightened if we do not purify our obscurations of mind and develop our wisdom potential. Therefore, no matter what teachings we hear, it is essential for each of us to try to actually *practice* these teachings, and to apply them to our lives in a practical way.

The Buddha said in his teachings, "I cannot take away the suffering of beings with my hands nor can I place my wisdom and realization in the hands of beings. That is not possible. What I can do instead is teach the method for attaining enlightenment that is without any error." The Buddha continued, "Whether or not a person is able to attain complete liberation, experience an end to suffering, and experience the total development of wisdom, will depend upon that person's effort in his or her practice." This means that even if two students receive the same teachings, one of them might develop faster due to superior diligence and motivation.

The profound teachings of the Buddha are actually a method that is presented in stages. We could say that the first stage is for the beginner, and is an entry point for the journey. The second stage is for those who have already made some progress, and the third stage is for those who are quite advanced. A particular approach or method goes along with each stage, and the methods build upon each other. It is like the fact that when we start off in life, our capacity is that of a child. As we enter into adulthood, our capacity increases, and we build on what we have learned. Then we become fully mature, and have the experience and wisdom of a lifetime. We must progress through the steps of the Buddha's teachings in much the same manner.

There are some people, however, who lack confidence in their abilities, and feel they should remain at the beginning level of practice all their lives. There are also people who think they should start right out by practicing at the highest level. Neither is possible. When you are completely new to Dharma, you need to be introduced to the teachings and practice at the most basic level. Once you have experience with that, you do not remain at the beginning stage, but go on to progressively more advanced stages of practice and study.

We all have to follow this system in order to develop ourselves. The image of building a house is a useful analogy in order to understand this process: we may want to put on the roof first because we are eager to finish the house, but this is not possible without the walls and the foundation. Therefore, we have to begin with the foundation, and then put up the walls, and finally the roof.

The next question is: How do we practice the method? We need to approach each teaching in a definite sequence: first by listening, then contemplating, and finally, meditating.

Listening to the teachings is most traditionally done in person, with a qualified teacher. It also includes studying books such as this one. The idea that listening or study comes first does not mean we must become familiar with every single Buddhist teaching, which would obviously take a very long time. It simply means that we need to be open and absorb the teachings we receive. What is the best way to take it in? Traditionally, this first phase is said to be like taking medicine from a trusted doctor. If you are sick and a doctor gives you medicine, you simply take it. You do not have to learn all about medicine before taking a treatment, and indeed that would be quite impractical.

In this way, listening openly to the teachings that are given is the first step. However—and this is a very important point—this does not mean accepting the teachings with blind faith. In fact, the Buddhist tradition, starting with the Buddha himself, has always discouraged blind faith. Nevertheless, we have to have the openness and diligence to actually absorb the teachings that are presented, and that is what is meant by listening.

The second step is contemplation. The Tibetan term for this is *sam*, which really just means to think. What we are calling contemplation here means thinking over what you have heard, pondering it, and considering if it is true, valid, and useful to you. It is a very personal process.

It is essential to contemplate the teachings you have heard because when you reflect on them, you keep them fresh in your memory. That is the only way you can integrate them into your own experience. As well, recollection of the vital points is essential when we go on to the next stage, which is meditation practice. If you skip the contemplation stage, you will be like a child who has been taken to see a movie. The child may enjoy the movie very much and may remember enjoying it, but he or she may soon forget the details of the plot, and in time will perhaps forget the movie altogether. We should not let ourselves forget the teachings because we did not reflect upon them after we heard them.

We should also think about the lineage or source of the teachings. Where did they come from? And what is the possible result of putting such teachings into practice? Asking these kinds of questions will help us investigate their validity, and give a context for their importance.

It bears repeating that blind faith is not the Buddhist approach. Only when you have tested and questioned the teachings in your own mind, and really thought about their validity, will you develop the kind of confidence you need to put them into practice. Though faith has a role in Buddhism, what is really needed is *understanding*. When confidence and certainty about the truth of a particular teaching dawns on you through contemplation, then it becomes useful and valid in your own experience. This certainty cuts through doubts. It is important to keep in mind, however, that this takes some work and patience.

Usually we have a sort of vague idea of what contemplation is. We say, "I'm in a contemplative mood." It is fine to do that, but the contemplation being discussed here is more specific. It means thinking over a specific teaching you have heard in a focused manner, analyzing it and turning it over in your mind in the ways we have discussed.

You may have heard about or seen Tibetan monastic debate, which is very colorful and even entertaining. Actually, this is part of the contemplation process. By testing each other in a very sharp and energetic way, the monks develop their skills in understanding and expressing the teachings. In the same way, a question and answer session at a teaching or a discussion group on Buddhism are ways that we can engage with this process. However, contemplation is fundamentally something you can and should do alone, working with your own mind.

As important as these first two steps of listening and contemplating are, we need to put what we have heard and contemplated into actual practice. That is the third stage, which is meditating. Without practice, listening and contemplating will not really benefit us. It is like learning to cook: a great chef may teach us what food to cook, how to prepare it, and even describe the taste of the food. However, if we never actually cook the food, we will still be hungry. The chef's teachings will not benefit us if we do not apply them. We have to cook to enjoy the meal, and that is the way meditation practice functions in Buddhism.

Therefore, to experience and enjoy the understanding, wisdom, and compassion that can grow within ourselves, we need to practice meditation. Meditation has often been misrepresented in the Western world, and the term alone has sometimes discouraged people. There are various misconceptions about meditation: for instance, some people think meditation is only for beginners and is not necessary once you are more advanced. However, meditation is an essential part of the spiritual journey, and is necessary for both beginners and advanced practitioners. Others think that meditating means they must go to an isolated place like a cave, abstain from eating, or practice other austerities. They think that meditating means giving up everything: family, home, possessions, and wealth.

With such views, the idea of meditation naturally intimidates people. However, these notions are not accurate. Becoming a practitioner of meditation does not mean that you have to give up everything. Instead, the practical approach that is recommended is to integrate meditation practice into our normal daily lives. Then, slowly and gradually, our spiritual strength and wisdom will develop.

This is not to say, however, that we will not experience changes once we begin meditating. As we develop our inner qualities, we naturally lessen our attachment to worldly concerns as well as material possessions. This detachment happens very naturally; we do not have to force ourselves to give up anything. As we develop, we will shed our attachment to possessions and worldly busyness as easily as we shed our heavy winter clothes when winter changes to spring. It is also similar to going from a hostile country to a friendly one: we do not hesitate to leave the first country and go toward the more appealing one. The changes you experience with practice are natural and comfortable because they happen along with your inner development.

Without this inner development, giving up things is very unpleasant. Take the example of the Tibetan refugees who, without any choice, had to leave their mother country. The transition from Tibet to India was uncomfortable for some of them because they had not sufficiently developed their inner qualities and were deeply attached to their land. However, with the development of inner qualities, this does not happen. In fact, giving up things can actually be very pleasant.

Some people even think that meditation will cause mental problems. I can assure you that if you depend upon an authentic teacher and practice, it will not lead to any such difficulties. However, if you try meditating on your own without a teacher, or if you try to practice based only on learning through books, anything is possible. That actually could lead to all sorts of negative complications.

Trying to practice without proper guidance can be compared to reading a book about an interesting country. Having read the book, you start walking in what you think is the correct direction. You might be walking in a completely wrong direction, but it is impossible for the book to speak up and correct your path. Similarly, practicing meditation on your own could lead you in wrong directions. Instead, if we read about a fascinating country, we should try to get information from someone who has already been there. We should obtain directions and receive guidance, and then nothing will go wrong. We can get to that marvelous land, but experienced guidance is necessary. This is why connecting with an experienced teacher is important.

Another misconception people have about meditation is that it is somehow in conflict with worldly activities or worldly success. In fact, meditation helps an individual be successful in worldly activities as well as spiritual ones. Through meditation we learn how to relax and experience peace of mind. With this peacefulness also comes a joyful frame of mind. Because of this inner peace, we are able to deal with others without frustration or aggression, and always keep a positive state of mind. When others experience our peaceful qualities, they automatically like being in our presence.

Therefore, through learning how to maintain peace of mind, we are better able to deal with the difficult aspects of everyday life. Meditation also helps because through practice we develop wisdom, and wisdom is of course necessary in everything we do. By developing peace of mind and a kind heart through practice, it has been said by realized beings that you will become "the darling of the world." In short, you will be well-loved by everyone, which is to be very successful indeed.

Practicing kindness and compassion will bring happiness not only to you, but to those around you as well. You become more willing to listen to others' problems and better able to help them. If someone tries to share their problems with you when you are depressed or upset, you may be unable to listen to them, or even become angry at them and say harsh or hurtful things. Yet this never happens when you mind is peaceful and happy. Mental peacefulness helps you do everything better. If your mind is peaceful, you can do whatever task you undertake without mistakes. Mental peace and tranquility are necessary in all activities, whether worldly or spiritual.

Another misconception about meditation is that many people are impatient with it and expect the results to come overnight. That is not possible. It is a process of development in which consistency is the key. Regular practice every day, even for a short period of time, is the proper way to progress from the beginning. If you practice for many hours a day at first and then drop the practice for months, there will be no development at all. An example I use for this is traveling in Tibet. In the remote parts of my country there are no cars, buses, or trains, and people have to travel mostly by foot. Cultivating a meditation practice is like walking somewhere on foot. If you begin walking and keep walking, even a very slow pace will sooner or later bring you to your destination. If you take long rests then jump up and start running you are more likely to exhaust yourself and never get where you are going.

If you keep practicing, you will definitely progress. Qualities of meditation experience will develop within you. But this cannot happen overnight. It happens the same way as humans grow: we come into this world as babies and grow up gradually. We are not born as a fully developed human being. We have to be patient and experience things as we grow. In the normal course of things, once we are born, we will grow up to be adults. Likewise, if we practice meditation regularly, we will certainly mature and develop our spiritual qualities.

This has been a short introduction to the profound potential and qualities we all have within ourselves, and to the Buddhist approach for unfolding those qualities. The method includes listening to the teachings, contemplating them, practicing meditation, and finally coming to the result which is the experience of our awakened qualities. Along the way you will find that this method helps in every part of your life as you continue toward the greater result, which is complete enlightenment.

Meditation Essentials

The Purpose of Meditation Practice

The purpose of meditation is to experience the awakened nature of the mind, and how we go about this process is at the very heart of the Buddhist way. To explore this essential subject, let's look at the Tibetan term *nangpa sangye*. *Nangpa* means inner, and *sangye* means enlightenment or the awakened state.

Nangpa, or inner, refers to our inner state of mind. In order to experience physical gentleness, calm, and well-being, we must first tame our rough, neurotic patterns of thought. By pacifying thoughts, we naturally will come to be more gentle, skillful, and free from aggression in our speech and our physical actions. This inner practice not only subdues confusion and brings about a peaceful, joyful state of mind, but it also makes the unfolding of enlightenment possible. In other words, developing inner tranquility makes it possible to experience the awakened state. The development of this peace is possible when the proper causes and conditions are present, which we will talk about later on.

The idea of enlightenment is intriguing, but it is easy to misunderstand. If we expect that enlightenment will simply be handed to us the way someone gives us a gift, we have missed the point. According to the Dharma, enlightenment is only possible through our own efforts. Even if we have received the necessary teachings, whether or not we achieve enlightenment depends upon our diligence.

We can better understand what is meant by enlightenment by breaking down the Tibetan term *sangye* into its two syllables. Sang means purification, and gye means development or blossoming. The process of purification means removing the faults and limitations which are all related to our ignorance. This means completely transcending confusion, delusions, and the negative mental patterns such as aggression, jealousy, attachment, and so on. These negative patterns are called kleshas in Sanskrit, and we will use the English term "mental afflictions" when we talk about them in more detail later on. After eliminating all of these mental afflictions, we may ask, "What's next? What happens in the absence of ignorance and confusion?" That is where *gye*, blossoming or development, occurs. When confusion is absent, the powers of the mind are perfected, and wisdom and insight develop. We also develop diligence, diligence in developing ourselves as well as in working for others. Therefore enlightenment includes the elimination of all faults and the development of qualities and virtues, and we can achieve this through practicing meditation.

There are three principles used in the teaching tradition of Buddhism that can help us see how the process of development takes place in meditation. The principles are known as ground, path, and fruition. The ground refers to the basis or beginning point, and here it means our own potential for enlightenment. Path refers to the process of engaging in practice. Fruition means the final outcome or result. With consistent practice, the experience of spiritual awakening will come about. That is the fruition that is possible for us based on our inherent potential for enlightenment (ground) and the correct application of practice (path).

In Tibetan Buddhism, the path of meditation and the spiritual journey in general is presented in three broad types of methods, which are known as the three *yanas*. Yana is a Sanskrit term that means a path or vehicle, a way of getting from here to there. In this case, the "here" is our ordinary confused state, and the path or yana is a particular way of progressing toward awakening. The three yanas are known as hinayana, mahayana, and vajrayana.

It may seem that because there are three different paths, there are also three different results. Actually, the Tibetan tradition integrates these three paths, which function as the beginning, intermediate, and advanced stages of the journey toward the fruition, which is supreme awakening. Thus it is important to point out that although there are three different paths, there are not three different results.

If that is so, you may ask, "Why are three paths necessary? Why not make it simple and have just one path?" There are three paths because human beings do not always have the same level of mental and spiritual sophistication. Ultimately they do, but practically speaking, at any given time some people are extremely sharp and advanced, others are somewhat less so, and others are not particularly well developed at all. Because of this, teachings are given in accordance with an individual's capacity to grasp the meaning. There is no point presenting the highest teachings to those who cannot understand them.

The different types of human capacity are like the different capacities of an infant, a child, and an adult, and the different paths are like different types of food. If we tried to feed adult food to an infant, the baby would probably not survive because infants need milk. If you were to feed an older child only milk, it would not be right for her because she needs solid food in her diet. And feeding only milk or a child's portion of food to an adult would not work either because adults need larger portions of solid food. Three different types and amounts of food are required because individuals are at different stages of development. Similarly, there are three different paths because people's capacity to understand and practice is also different.

In the same way, if you are practicing the hinayana (often called the "lesser vehicle"), you must not think that this will always be sufficient. It is like the previous example in which an infant drinks milk, then grows to be a child who needs solid food as well as milk, and then becomes an adult who eats only solid food. In the same way, although we start by practicing the lesser vehicle, we will go on to the greater vehicle (mahayana) and highest vehicle (vajrayana) in order to experience full enlightenment.

Whether someone is of the highest, middle, or lesser capacity, the path to enlightenment starts with the practice of calm-abiding meditation. This is called shamata in Sanskrit, which simply means "tranquility." This type of practice is also often just called "sitting meditation." Shamata meditation is necessary for all three types of individuals because normally we are subject to constant distraction and we are totally caught up in our stream of thoughts. Such a practice is a necessary first step on the journey because it helps develop concentration and the ability to let go of thoughts.

All three types of people require calm-abiding meditation in the same way that all good writers started out by learning the alphabet as children. Based on that, they were able to go on to become accomplished writers later in life. If they had not learned the basics of reading and writing, they could not possibly have developed in that way. Similarly, learning basic sitting meditation is essential for all three types of people. Some will then go on to the highest practices, but in any case, everyone needs the foundation.

Although calm-abiding meditation is the foundation of all meditation practices, there is an even more general foundation for Dharma practice overall, which is ethical development. To understand this, let's consider the following four-line stanza of teachings by the Buddha. In these four simple statements we can see the essential characteristics of Dharma and the purpose of meditation.

Commit no negative actions whatsoever
Practice virtue perfectly
Pacify your mind completely
This is Buddhadharma

The first statement is "Commit no negative actions whatsoever." "Negative actions" means actions that are harmful. According to the truth of cause and effect, if we do something that harms beings, we will experience suffering as a result. There is nothing pleasant or positive about such an act, and that is why it is said to be negative. According to this statement, we must not only avoid some negative actions, but all such activities completely.

All beings wish to experience happiness, peace, and success, and to be free from suffering and pain. But although we try to obtain happiness, almost no one experiences the complete fulfillment of that wish. The reason for this is that they do not know that negative actions lead to failure and misfortune and that virtuous activities lead to success, confidence, and fulfillment. Not knowing this, they engage in activities blindly and with confusion, and as a result of their confusion, they constantly make mistakes.

We ourselves are the ones who experience the results of our actions. If you engage in an evil activity, you are the one who is subject to the painful outcome of the karmic cause and effect relationship that action creates. If a hungry person eats poisonous food, who is going to suffer? The one who eats the food is the one who suffers, and this is true regardless of the person's intentions.

Similarly, being confused and acting with incomplete awareness, we are bound to make mistakes and harm other beings, and we will experience the negative results of that action. As well, if we practice virtue and accumulate merit, we experience good fortune. Whoever engages in an activity, whether positive or negative, is the one who experiences the result. There are positive results from positive activities, and negative results from negative activities. The results of our negative or positive actions are not given to us by someone, nor can they be taken away from us.

At this point you may think, "I accept that the result of negative actions is to experience pain, but how can I really be sure that I do not engage in them?" The answer is to be mindful of three basic things: your behavior, your speech, and your thoughts. If you are careful about these three points, you can avoid all non-virtuous activities.

It may seem that our body and its behavior is what are most powerful because it is our body that engages in actions such as violence. If we look at this in a more subtle way, however, it becomes clear that the body is not the most powerful aspect of our being, nor is speech. Instead, the mind is the most powerful. For example, if we do not have angry thoughts, we will not speak in an angry way or take actions based on that. If we do have anger in the mind, then we will tend to speak in accordance with that, and possibly act on it as well. Therefore, body and speech simply follow the ideas that originate in the mind.

Another way to look at this is to think that if the body was the most powerful thing, then a corpse would be very powerful. However, the fact is that a dead body cannot do anything. In the absence of mind, the body is helpless. Therefore, mind is the most important aspect of our being, and that is why pacifying the mind is the first thing emphasized in Buddhism.

The second statement is "Practice virtue perfectly." Now, when you are told, "Do not commit any negative actions whatsoever, and practice virtue perfectly," you may ask, "How could I possibly do that? What do I have to do to avoid all evil and practice virtue—and not only practice it, but do so perfectly?" The answer is that we can progress toward this ideal by developing the precise mindfulness that comes about from meditation. By combining that with a clear and honest understanding of positive and negative actions (these will be covered in the next section), we can find our way to live our lives properly and act in a way that is most beneficial and auspicious.

In a very real way, these first two steps are inseparable from the third statement, which is "Pacify your mind completely." This is what is possible by achieving the fruition of meditation practice. Practicing meditation brings about the precise mindfulness, tranquility, and awareness that make it possible to avoid all negativity and engage in authentic virtue.

Exactly how is it that pacifying the mind and developing the tranquility of calm abiding leads to practicing perfect virtue and freedom from all negativity?" The answer is that developing in these ways allows us to come out from under the cloud, so to speak, of our confusion and mental afflictions. All our confusion and mental afflictions are based on ignorance, which is our primary problem. Arising from that, we all have a lot of attachment and grasping, and out of this we create all sorts of difficult and painful situations. In the absence of attachment, however, it is possible to have perfect discipline of body, speech, and mind. Also arising from ignorance is the basic pattern of aggression and hatred, and it is quite clear what the result of that is. However, in the absence of hatred, we will have patience and tolerance. Pacifying the mind allows us to cut through our ignorance, attachment, and hatred. In the absence of ignorance and the associated mental afflictions, there is no confusion, and without confusion, there is wisdom and insight. This enables us to practice virtue perfectly.

When you first encounter such an idea, it may be difficult to believe—and in fact it may not even make sense. It may seem that the elimination of all mental afflictions—all confusion, mistakes, ignorance, attachment, hatred, or anger —would be impossible. However, the reason this seems impossible is that all our lives we have been controlled by mental afflictions.

For example, imagine a man has been locked inside a dark, windowless house for many years. Then someone comes in and tells him that outside the house there is sunshine, as well as beautiful flowers and trees. But the man is unable to see the light and beauty of the outside world no matter hard he looks from inside the dark house. At the same time, to assume that those things do not exist would not be correct. He might wonder how he could experience the outside world, and would consider trying to make a hole in the wall to see what is outside.

Simply knowing or hearing that there is a world outside the walls does not make the walls go away. The man needs to put forth some effort. Without any special tools, he would have to try to make a hole in the wall by hand. It could take years. However, if he never gave up, one day he would be able to make a hole in the wall and see the sunshine and the beauty of the outside world.

In the same way, because of the walls of our obscurations and mental afflictions, the possibility of enlightenment may be difficult to accept. However, this should not prevent us from practicing meditation.

The fourth statement is "This is Buddhadharma." The reason for this statement is that the Buddha did not differentiate between those who follow his tradition and those who do not based upon outer appearances. The essential quality of a genuine practitioner of Dharma is not something external, such as shaving your head or wearing robes. In the same way, wearing your hair long and wearing ordinary clothes does not mean that you are not a Buddhist. It does not depend on being male or female, or whether you have high or low status in society.

The actual practice of Dharma consists of training your mind, engaging in positive activities, and avoiding negative activities of body, speech, and mind, and working to cut through ego fixation. As well, if you develop an altruistic mind, an attitude of wanting to benefit others, then you are in keeping with Buddhism regardless of anything external.

Each of us needs to be the true witness of whether or not we are authentic practitioners of Dharma. No one else can make that judgment; we have to look at ourselves based upon how we really live our lives. When you have applied the Buddhist teachings to your life for a little while, you can review your situation and examine what sort of changes have happened since you met with the Dharma. By this I mean changes in your state of mind and emotions, not particularly in your lifestyle. Then you can form an opinion as to whether you have been a genuine practitioner, and whether the practices you have applied have helped you or not.

This may not be obvious under ordinary circumstances, but you will learn more about whether these practices have helped you when you meet with adverse conditions. Someone may boast about his strength, but he can only find out if he is strong by lifting heavy things. In the same way, a man may say he is a fearless warrior, but to find out if that is really true you would have to see how he acts in battle. Therefore, until we meet with adverse conditions, we may not really know how we have changed. But when you do meet with adverse conditions, you can see how you react.

You have to be gentle with yourself about this, and realistic. It is not about expectations. We all have confusion and *kleshas*, but do adverse conditions affect you more or less than in the past? Are your patterns of aggression, jealousy, and so on raging out of control, or have they weakened? This is very personal, because you need to look back to how you were when you first encountered the Dharma, and compare that to how you are at present. If adverse conditions seem to affect you less than when you first met with the Dharma, then the practice has been a help to you and you are doing it properly. In this way you can witness your own development, and know in a very personal way whether your practice has been genuine not.

Meditation Practice Instructions

We have talked in general about the importance of meditation practice and how it fits into the Buddhist path. Now I would like to give you some specific information about the practice of basic sitting meditation, or shamata. However, you need to understand from the start that the proper approach to developing a meditation practice is to get guidance in person from a qualified instructor, and to continue interacting with teachers and instructors such that you can get feedback on what you are experiencing, have your questions answered, and so on. At the same time, if you are interested in meditation it is entirely appropriate to study and investigate what it is all about, as long as you appreciate the need for personal instruction.

As I have said, shamata is a Sanskrit term that means tranquility or peace. In Tibetan the term for shamata is *shinay*. The first syllable, *shi*, means peace or pacification. In this context it means the pacification or reduction of the power of the thoughts and all the mental events that continuously take place in our minds. It is not that thoughts will entirely cease, but their power is lessened. The second syllable, nay, means to abide. This means that through the generation of tranquility, we gain the ability to let the mind rest on a chosen object for as long as we wish, whether it is an imagined object or something perceived, such as the breath.

There are many different approaches to practicing shamata, and many different methods that can be used. However, what all these methods have in common is the aim of lessening the power of conceptual fixation and being able to bring the mind to rest one-pointedly.

Shamata is not just a Buddhist practice. It is practiced by many spiritual traditions because it is the necessary basis for any kind of spiritual development. However, there are some differences between its application in the Buddhist tradition and other traditions, and therefore differences in the qualities that result.

Let's consider the causes and conditions that are needed for proper shamata meditation. According to the approach that is taught in the traditional Buddhist texts, the basic set of conditions is to be in a place of solitude so that distractions are minimal, and to sit on a comfortable and stable seat with crossed legs. Then, with an erect posture, you place your mind in a state of tranquility. This attention to place, posture, and so forth forms the root of the conditions for the Buddhist practice of shamata.

There are many different explanations of shamata practice which describe particular ways of removing the defects that inhibit practice, the arising of qualities associated with the practice, and its final result. For instance, the Third Gyalwa Karmapa, Rangjung Dorje, stated:

The waves of subtle and gross thoughts subside by themselves.
The waters of unmoving mind rest naturally.
May the ocean of shamata
Be undisturbed, free from the dregs of drowsiness.

The first line, "the waves of subtle and gross thoughts subside by themselves," describes the removal of faults. Then the next line, "the waters of unmoving mind rest naturally," describes the qualities of a stable mind. Finally, the result or fruition is described as an aspiration: "May the ocean of shamata be undisturbed, free from the dregs of drowsiness." This verse explains the basic approach to shamata meditation. We will investigate and explain this in more detail as we go along.

ABIDING IN SOLITUDE

The first point that is traditionally emphasized is abiding in solitude. Solitude refers to both external and internal isolation. External isolation consists of practicing in a place where you are not going to be disturbed in some way. This means being free from the type of anxiety you would experience when there is some sort of threat or uncertainty in your practice environment. A proper location for meditation would be one where it is appropriate for you to be. For example you would not be trespassing or intruding on a place that others wanted to use for some other purpose. As well, the building you are using would not be about to fall down or harm you in some way. In general, external isolation means to be in a practice environment where you are in control of the situation, a place where you have freedom from danger or disturbance.

Internal isolation consists of not allowing yourself to be seduced by thoughts. If you sit in an appropriate environment with the proper posture, but still allow your mind to wander and be pulled around by arising thoughts, that is not the correct practice of shamata. Just sitting in a meditation posture is not enough. The thoughts that arise can be classified as thoughts of the past, thoughts of the present, and thoughts of the future. Usually, we are remembering and analyzing the past, or thinking about what we are doing right now (or what we might be doing right now). Or else we could be thinking about what might happen in the future and making all kinds of plans. If we let ourselves be caught in one of these types of thought processes, this is not correct meditation practice. In order to acquire inner isolation, we must rely upon an appropriate technique in order to cool down or pacify our minds.

HAVING A COMFORTABLE AND STABLE SEAT

The next important point is having a comfortable and stable seat. This is really quite important because when we meditate we cannot sit on something that will distract us. The seat should not be too hard or too soft. To relieve strain on your back, whatever you sit on should make your backside a little bit higher than your knees.

In addition, you should not be tilted to the right or left, because constantly compensating for being tilted would also cause strain and distraction. Having a proper seat is also important because it allows the upper body to be straight and erect. Most meditation centers have good cushions to sit on, and most people who do meditation at home get their own cushion for that. It is important that the seat is right for you, however, so you need to investigate your own needs.

THE FIVE BASIC POINTS OF POSTURE

These five positions explain the correct meditative posture for meditation. They describe a way of positioning the body so the mind naturally comes to rest in a state of comfort, and as a result your mind's true nature is naturally revealed. Note that there are some variations of this posture that are taught for more advanced practices. However, what is being explained here is a very basic set of principles of posture that will be pretty much the same in any Buddhist approach to meditation.

THE FIRST POSITION: THE LEGS

The first of the aspects of correct posture is that the legs are crossed. If you are flexible enough, you should sit in what is called vajra posture, with the feet placed on the opposite thighs. This is also known as the full lotus position. If this is too difficult for you, you can sit with one leg in front of the other in what is called the bodhisattva posture. Either one is correct.

In the basic traditional explanation that describes shamata practice, it says that the legs should be crossed, and it is not really much more specific than that. The point is that the posture should give you a stable seat: you are not going to fall to the right or left, and there is no strain in staying upright.

THE SECOND POSITION: THE HANDS

The second part is the position of the hands. Place one hand in the palm of the other and place them facing up below your navel. An alternate position is to rest the hands palms down on the thighs above the knees.

THE THIRD POSITION: KEEPING A STRAIGHT BACK

The third part of taking the posture corrects the tendency to be somewhat hunched over as a result of the hand placement. Rather than contracting your stomach, which tends to cause you to bend over, first push your stomach out, then relax and sit back a little bit without displacing the position of the hands. This prevents you from leaning forward and slumping over. The back and shoulders should be erect but not tense in meditation.

THE FOURTH POSITION: THE GAZE

The first three steps take care of the posture from the shoulders down, but we have not yet taken care of the neck and head. The next step is to direct your gaze. You begin by looking in the direction of the tip of your nose with both eyes, and then extending that gaze straight out in that direction, which results in your gaze coming to rest at a point on the ground about a foot and a half in front of your legs. This gaze will prevent you from moving your neck from side to side, bending it back and looking up, or bending it forward and looking too far down.

THE FIFTH POSITION: THE POSITION OF THE CHIN

The fifth and last point is to push the chin down a little so it presses down lightly on your throat. The point of this is not to stick your chin up. If you pull your chin in correctly, your spine will be quite straight through your upper back and neck.

These aspects of posture will give you a straight posture that enables the mind to rest easily. It is a bit like a vessel filled with water: if the vessel is left undisturbed, the water inside will just sit there without any waves.

These positions have both outer and inner benefits. At this point I have explained the outer benefits; the inner benefits are concerned with the higher levels of practice, and you will come to understand those benefits when you undertake those levels.

THE DEVELOPMENT OF SHAMATA: OBJECTS OF FOCUS

The next aspect of the development of shamata is to place your mind in a meditative state, or samadhi. Samadhi means meditative absorption, and it refers to bringing the mind to rest on one chosen object. Sometimes the object of meditation is also called a "support" because it supports the focusing of the mind. There are many different objects that can be used to develop basic shamata. For example, it could be something neutral that is easy to look at for a long time, such as a small rock or stick. You simply place such an object in front of you and direct your attention to it. You can also use a statue of the Buddha or a stupa. You can use written letters or syllables, the most common being AH or HUM. You can also use dots, such as a drawing of a dot in any color.

In all these cases, you direct your eyes to a support that is physically present. Because your eyes are directed to that object, your mind naturally comes to rest upon it as well. This makes use of our tendency to be involved with visual perception.

BREATHING AS AN OBJECT OF FOCUS

Another approach is to direct your attention to your breathing. This is done naturally; your breathing is not manipulated, regulated, lengthened, or shortened in any way. Simply direct your attention to the breathing. When your mind becomes attentive to the process of breathing, it starts to come to rest.

The main approach that I teach is to direct your attention to the breath, which in this case means both the out-breath and the in-breath. The reason for using this technique is that the natural presence of the breath and its movement in and out is a relatively easy way to pacify thoughts. The movement of the thoughts becomes coordinated with the exhalation and inhalation, and everything starts to cool down and slow down.

If you are using the approach of directing attention to your breathing, always start with an inhalation. Although in general you do not try to manipulate the breath in any way, at the beginning take a very long, slow breath. This gives you a fresh start, uninhibited by any chain of thoughts that may have started before the session. To do this, after taking your posture, inhale slowly and feel the breath going in and going down below the navel. Then when you exhale that first time, feel the breath going out and dissipating into space. This initial slow breath is very helpful for beginning shamata practitioners in order to cool down their thoughts.

In the beginning it is helpful to have a continuous support, which in this case is the breath, and that is why I recommend the technique of directing the attention to both cycles of the breath, the inhalation and exhalation.

When you are starting the practice, you will tend to get lost in thought and lose the focus on the breath. Once you recognize that you have become distracted, that you are thinking, just return to the breath. And when you return to the breath, you can start fresh the way you did at the beginning of the session by taking a long breath in and a long breath out. This is extremely helpful in cutting through the chain of conceptuality.

When a practitioner has been doing this for some time and has become so used to it that the mind naturally rests with the breathing, the next step is to simply maintain a bare recognition of the breathing process. Rather than following the breath all the way in and out, just have a light sense of the breath going in and out through the nose, nothing more detailed than that. Let go of any thoughts about the breath, and just feel it at the nostrils.

It is a sign of good shamata practice if your mind can rest on whatever object it is placed, but this will not happen quickly, so don't develop expectations in that regard.

PRACTICE EXPERIENCES

When you first start to practice shamata, you will probably find that you are more comfortable when you are not meditating than when you are. This is because when you meditate your mind seems to be filled with more thought and conceptuality than before, and when you are not meditating everything seems fine.

This happens because before you started meditating your mind was more directed to your sensory perceptions, and as a result you did not recognize all the thoughts that were always running through your mind. On the other hand, when you are sitting and directing your attention solely to the simple technique, you experience thoughts that interrupt the experience of non-distraction. Therefore you should not think that your mind is getting worse! In fact, the recognition of thoughts and the discomfort of that recognition is a very good sign, because it means that you are starting to acknowledge them. It is a little bit like a big field with a wide stream running through it: the water might not seem to be moving very fast, but if it gets channeled into a narrower stream, the current seems quite swift. It is not that there is actually any more water flowing; it is just that the current is more obvious because it is concentrated in one place.

Practitioners tend to have a sequence of experiences when practicing shamata. The first is that your mind seems like a waterfall, an unimpeded, extremely loud sequence of thoughts, as if water were being forced over the edge of a cliff. There seems to be no peace, but actually this is good because you are simply seeing what has been going on all along. Recognizing the waterfall is the first step to cooling down the mind.

Next, your mind starts to be more like a river flowing fast over a level surface. Sometimes the river is turbulent and sometimes it is not. In the same way, sometimes the mind will be disturbed by thoughts and other times it seems to be cooling down.

The third experience that occurs for practitioners is that while thoughts continue to arise, they are not particularly a problem; they do not distract you from your chosen object of meditation. This is like an ocean that is constantly full of waves, yet the waves do not pose a problem for the ocean. They do not displace the water; they simply arise and then go back into the ocean. This experience indicates an advanced level of shamata, and it is a very good sign because it means that you are starting to be trained.

The fourth type of experience is when simply by taking the correct posture, your mind cools down immediately due to the habit and practice of meditation. In this case, simply sitting down to meditate is the technique. You do not have to try to force the mind into the grid of the technique, because your mind naturally remains at rest wherever it is placed. You do not have to pull your mind in or push your mind out, because it simply stays put. You are not disturbed by thoughts, and you are not disturbed by perceptions. This fourth experience is like an ocean with no waves, and it is what is referred to in the Third Karmapa's verse about shamata practice where he refers to, "a stable ocean without the waves of torpor and excitement."

People who reach this level of shamata practice will be very calm, even if they had been previously unruly and aggressive. Whatever anxiety they may have had has given way to mental relaxation. Generally, no matter where such people are or what they doing, they will always be tranquil, subdued, and disciplined in conduct. People with that type of practice will not be especially delighted by pleasant experiences or conditions, and will not feel upset when unpleasant conditions or hassles arise. They are not controlled by external conditions because they have the inner stability of mental tranquility and ease. External conditions do not have much effect upon such people simply because they do not rely upon them.

You have to really continue with shamata practice until you get to this point. When your mind has been tamed to this extent, you have the basis for the practice of insight (vipasyana). This is because your mind will come to rest upon whatever object of meditation you chose. Also, at this point you can begin to work with the higher levels of practice because your mind is workable and will engage with any chosen object.

Therefore, if shamata is properly applied, it is the basis for the development of many desirable qualities. But if it is improperly applied, it can also be the basis for the development of defects. This is because as you start to cool down, you become more comfortable mentally, and this state of tranquility leads to real bliss. It is possible to enjoy this bliss so much that you fixate on it as the goal of practice. You become like a cat being scratched behind the ears; you go into the experience of ease and pleasure further and further. When you fall prey to this kind of fixation, then unfortunately the more shamata practice you do, the more stable your meditation and the deeper your fixation. As a result, anything that takes you away from that indulgent tranquility is seen as threatening, and you generate an aggression proportionate to your fixation. Most types of meditation lead to this.

Since it is necessary to develop shamata, the only way to transcend this dangerous sidetrack is to completely let go of whatever happens when you are meditating. No matter how good you feel, do not attempt to own that or perpetuate the experience. Do not to make a goal of it, and simply let go of it.

THE DEFECTS OF TORPOR AND EXCITEMENT

Torpor and excitement are defects that are impediments to the development of shamata as well as any other kind of meditation practice. Torpor occurs in meditation when you find that your body starts to feel weak, as if you could not move even if you wanted to. Your mind also starts to feel unclear, without any kind of perky clarity. You might actually fall asleep at this point, but even if you do not fall asleep, your mind is dull. You may not be particularly disturbed by thoughts and your mind may be fairly stable, but it is stable in a dull, sleepy way. As long as you remain in this state of torpor, you will not receive any benefit from shamata practice.

The second defect is excitement. This can manifest as the arising of thoughts related to the kleshas such as attachment or anger, or it can be some kind of attraction or irritation about the external environment. In either case, the problem with excitement is that it prevents you from settling your mind on the chosen object or technique. Often this happens in the following way: a mental affliction arises which causes you to direct your attention to an external object. You become so involved with that object or sense perception that you cannot bring yourself back to the technique even when you recognize that you have become distracted.

Torpor and excitement are the main obstacles to meditation practice. However, there are remedies for both. When you find that you are afflicted by torpor, the remedy is to literally bring everything upwards. This means that you focus the strength of your awareness and attention to posture, and you actually tighten everything up a bit. If possible, sit in the vajra posture and raise your gaze, looking upwards into the sky or into the space in front of you. Perhaps you can even tense your body a little bit, and with great care direct your attention to the technique. For example, you could follow the breath all the way in and all the way out, causing your awareness to focus one-pointedly on the technique. This will dispel torpor.

If you are practicing alone, another way to dispel torpor is to get up and practice walking meditation for a few minutes, paying great attention to your posture. This will break through your absorption in mental dullness. When you sit down again, it should be gone. If you are practicing with others, of course, you cannot just decide to do this but must wait for the appropriate time to get up.

If you find that you are becoming excited and cannot bring your mind back to the object or the technique, it is recommended to bring everything downwards. This means focusing your gaze downwards, and even bending down a little and closing your eyes so you create a sense of darkness. That will cool down the chain of excitement, and then after a couple of minutes you can straighten up again and return to normal.

Another approach recommended for dealing with these two defects is visualization. This approach is quite simple. In the case of torpor, when you breathe out imagine your breath as bright white light which floats up and dissolves into the space above you. When you breathe in, this white light comes in through the nostrils and fills your whole body. This visualization can dispel torpor. In the same way, if you fall prey to excitement, imagine as you breathe out that your breath is like black light, and this darkness sinks into the ground as a large mass which becomes narrower and narrower until it is gathered into a needle point that goes down into the ground. When you breathe in, think that your breath takes the form of black light that fills your body with darkness. This visualization helps to dispel the excitement.

It is necessary to rely on these remedies until the problem is resolved. There is not a certain amount of time you should do it, such as a certain number of breaths or minutes. You simply apply the remedy as needed until the torpor or excitement has been dispelled. However, if you find that there is so much torpor or excitement that no matter what remedy you apply you cannot break through it, you should stop practicing and do something else. This is because if you continue to practice within the state of torpor or excitement, you will perpetuate the habit of it. You should take a break, and do some physical work or anything else that might help you break through it.

Generally speaking, however, it is very important to be committed to your practice time period. For example, if you practice shamata regularly for one hour and have a firm commitment that you are not going to do anything for that hour other than shamata, you should not move until that hour is finished, no matter what. It is important to have this commitment—to have the attitude that, "This hour is the time to practice shamata. I'm not going to think about my other responsibilities, what I have to do afterwards, what I did before, or anything else." This commitment forms the basis for generating tranquility, so it is of tremendous benefit.

If you have this kind of commitment, then your mind will naturally settle down for your practice period, and obstacles to practice will tend not to arise. If your commitment is weak, if you enter into a session of practice thinking, "Well, maybe I'll sit for an hour, but if I get uncomfortable, I'll get up and do something else," then naturally situations will arise either externally or internally that cause you to get up and do something else. Then there will not be much benefit from your meditation practice.

QUESTIONS AND ANSWERS

STUDENT: If my body begins to hurt while in the correct position but my mind wishes to continue the practice, is it all right to continue in a chair if it provides the correct support?

RINPOCHE: Usually this means that you are not used to practice. In that case, you just have to get used to it. Sometimes people have a specific illness or disability which prevents them from performing one part or another of the correct posture. In that case, they should obviously omit the part that they cannot physically perform and do the best they can. However, if there is nothing really wrong with you, if you can do it but it is just uncomfortable, then you have to get used to it gradually. The way to do that is to have short sessions of practice, then gradually your body will get used to it and you can prolong the sessions.

STUDENT: In this culture, we tend to be very hard on ourselves and judge the thoughts that come up as good or bad. I'm wondering how the natural process of relinquishing that judgment occurs.

RINPOCHE: You simply have to return to the breath. There really is no strategy you can use as an antidote to judging your thoughts. The point is that the hope and anxiety we have with regard to our thoughts, along with the judgments we engage in as a result of that hope and anxiety, are all just thoughts as well. They are just part of our thought stream and not something separate that must be treated as special.

As your shamata practice starts to stabilize, your thoughts become more transparent, and then your judgment, anxiety, and hope become more transparent as well. When you have stable shamata, you do not delight in pleasure or feel anguished at unpleasant conditions as much as you did before. This is because there is a stable calm in your mind, which means that you are less dependent upon external conditions. In the same way, when you start to practice a lot, you do not have to block thoughts or judge them because you do not have to reject your experience. Your natural tranquility renders you more and more impervious to the seduction of that judgment.

STUDENT: What is the correct position of the eyelids during meditation? Can they be half-closed, closed, or open? What are the benefits of each of these positions?

Rinpoche: I do not know in detail the benefits for different degrees of opening or closing the eyelids. However, in the case of beginners who find they are so caught up by visual perception they cannot direct their minds to an object, it is appropriate to close the eyes. Especially if you are prey to excitement, it is definitely better to meditate with the eyes closed until that excitement is dispelled. Otherwise it is best to allow the eyes to find their own natural degree of openness and closure.

When you are meditating, I suppose that generally the eyes are about half open, but it is not something that is done intentionally. You do not have to try to adjust the eyes so that they are exactly half-open. This advice is in the context of shamata level of practice. When you practice insight (vipasyana) meditation, there are very specific instructions for the gaze.

STUDENT: When I meditate I often experience strong physical sensations that seem linked to the ability to concentrate, and as the ability to concentrate dissipates, so do these physical sensations. It is just a lot of energy. Often it's as if I'm moving upward, with the energy generated from my feet and moving up through my body. It is like a sensation of being lifted upward and a loss of physical sensation. Is that linked to either torpor or excitement? Is it an appropriate experience?

RINPOCHE: Actually, it does not make any difference. It probably indicates that you are becoming slightly distracted; the sensations are not particularly helpful, but they are also not a problem. But no matter what kind of experience or sensation arises, simply return to the breath.

Many kinds of experiences arise in meditation practice. When any of them arise, it is appropriate to simply return to whatever technique you are applying and not get involved with the experience, not be delighted, frightened, or threatened in any way. If you do not become involved with these experiences and simply return to the technique, they can be helpful. On the other hand, if you become involved with them they can be a big problem.

STUDENT: Is it necessary that this state of shamata spoken of by the Third Karmapa be attained before attempting any other practice, such as visualization?

RINPOCHE: I think Chögyam Trungpa Rinpoche's approach to this question is the most helpful because, as he discovered, when people begin to practice Dharma they do not really have any certainty about it. When your certainty is still wavering, it is very easy to be distracted by any little pleasure or object that arises in your field of perception. This makes it impossible to do other practices such as visualization. For people in that situation, which seems to be basically the way things are in this country, it is very helpful to have a long period of shamata practice first. Then through that practice, your mind begins to cool down. Once your mind has cooled down, you can really understand the Dharma and gain certainty towards it. Then you can go on with other practices.

This is not the way it was done in Tibet, but because of the different cultural and social background, the situation there was slightly different. In Tibet, when people were exposed to what are called "the four thoughts which turn the mind,"[1] simply contemplating these thoughts generated intense sadness. This type of sadness cools you down and generates certainty in the Dharma. Having that certainty, they could go on and practice the *ngöndro*, the foundational practices for more advanced practice. Only after they had finished ngöndro were they allowed to practice shamata. Once they gained some facility with shamata, they were given the pointing out instructions, and then they were able to begin vipasyana. In the West it seems best for people to start shamata from the very beginning.

---

1   The four are the contemplation of (1) the preciousness of human life, (2) impermanence, (3) the law of karma, and (4) the defects of samsara.

STUDENT: What is the intention behind learning to focus on an object?

RINPOCHE: The purpose of directing the mind to an object or a technique is the cooling down and lessening of thought. The result is that you can direct your mind one-pointedly to any virtuous attitude or activity.

STUDENT: The state of tranquility in which one does not experience the extremes of emotion sounded very neutral to me, and I wonder if you could explain that.

RINPOCHE: Actually, that level of tranquility or stability is not what you could call a neutral state. This state of tranquility is characterized by an unshakable confidence. This means that you cannot be controlled or shaken by external conditions, and such a state really is not neutral at all.

Traditionally, neutrality means two different things: one is an action which is morally neutral, neither beneficial nor harmful to yourself or others, and the other is a state in which there is no sensation. This is a state where we do not remember or think of anything, and are somewhat insensate. Things do not become a bother because you are not aware of them. This second type of neutrality might be confused with meditative stability, but it is very different. In a state in which there is no sensation, you are not experiencing what is happening. In a state of meditative stability, you experience everything very precisely, but nothing is a big deal.

STUDENT: If you experience a sense of warmth and comfort in practice, can't this comfort become a trap?

RINPOCHE: There is no real danger that you will get attached to such sensations if you are still practicing and following the technique, which is being conscious of the breath. It could be a problem if you direct your attention to the sensations of warmth and comfort, but it is no more of a problem than directing your attention to any other sensation.

STUDENT: How does one combat intense drowsiness?

RINPOCHE: Have someone throw a bucket of water on you. Just kidding!

There are three situations which often bring about the intense desire to sleep when meditating. The first is if you have been working a lot and your body is tired. The second is if you have been eating a lot and all your energy is concentrated on digesting. The third is if it is too warm where you are practicing. Basically, the antidote to drowsiness is to raise your gaze and tighten up your posture.

STUDENT: Tensing your body?

RINPOCHE: You tense up for a bit because, generally speaking, the rigidity of the posture is maintained through mindfulness. There is no actual tension. You are not tensing your joints, for example. In this case, you shake yourself out of sleepiness by looking up and tensing your whole body for a few seconds.

The Benefits
of Shamata Practice

If you become trained in shamata practice, then you will be able to direct your attention to whatever Dharma practice you undertake. Because you have gained the ability to put your mind one-pointedly on whatever you chose, you will not become distracted no matter what you are practicing. All the practices you do will be workable and will yield the benefits associated with them. Correct shamata practice prepares you for insight because shamata cultivates the natural stability of mind which heightens its natural clarity. This brings forth your own intelligence, your own natural insight.

Some people have the misunderstanding that shamata practice is something you begin with and is not needed thereafter. That is not true. Shamata is the companion of all the vehicles of practice, and no Buddhist practice is possible without shamata. For example, in the mahayana tradition there are different sorts of samadhi or absorptions connected with the experience of loving-kindness and compassion. Although these absorptions are certainly the experience of these traits, they are nevertheless varieties of shamata. There is the shamata of loving-kindness and the shamata of compassion. In the vajrayana, of course, there are the visualization practices. These are also actually forms of shamata practice rather than being something different.

No matter what practice you do, your mind has to be able to abide within the technique or structure of that practice, and this abiding consists of and therefore depends upon the practice of shamata. Therefore, shamata is what enables you to accomplish the fruition of all the various stages of practice.

However, it is a mistake to think that shamata itself is enough. You cannot obtain buddhahood simply through shamata practice and, in fact, that is the difference between what are called supermundane and mundane practices. Mundane or worldly practice consists simply of shamata, and supermundane practice goes beyond that. You might wonder why I say that shamata is not enough after I have spent so much time extolling its benefits. Shamata weakens the kleshas to the point where other practices can occur, but it does not uproot the kleshas, and therefore it cannot bring you to awakening.

I have said that shamata has to be ripened into the experience of insight or vipasyana, but this does not happen automatically. It is not simply that shamata practice is somehow going to turn into vipasyana, because genuine insight only comes about through the removal of obscurations. Obscurations are removed only through the accumulation of merit and wisdom. If this were not the case, then we would only do shamata practice and not bother with more advanced practices, practices that bring about the accumulation of merit and wisdom.

It is necessary to rely upon an approach to Dharma which makes use of the qualities arising from shamata practice in order to gather the accumulation of merit and wisdom, and thereby generate the wisdom that has insight into the ultimate nature of the mind. When we talk about beginners practicing vipasyana meditation, we are really talking about concordant vipasyana, which is to say, something similar to real vipasyana. But until we have gathered a large amount of merit and removed our obscurations to a very significant degree, we cannot really practice vipasyana in the full sense of the word.

So far, we have discussed how shamata practice is necessary as the support for all Dharma practices, and the relationship of shamata to the experience of genuine insight or vipasyana. The fact that it functions as a support and basis for all higher practices, and specifically for vipasyana, is the benefit of shamata from a spiritual or dharmic point of view. However, shamata practice also has immediate benefits that can be experienced by a practitioner. Generally speaking, a lot of our suffering is due to our immediate reaction to the conditions we meet. We could say that we have no patience, no fortitude, and not much courage. The result of a stable shamata practice is that our minds become tamed and we become happier. This happiness and peace is something that does not really depend upon external conditions. It consists of having less neurotic thoughts and being less easily moved by the conditions we encounter. In other words, because fear is just a thought, we experience less fear. This means that we are not disturbed even in situations which we usually considered anxiety producing, and we find everything much easier to deal with.

The other benefit is that we are less distracted. Generally, when we do things, we make a lot of mistakes. In general, the mistakes we make come from distraction, from not directing our attention properly to what we are doing. The nature of shamata is that we are not distracted. The mind abides one-pointedly on whatever we are doing, whether it is Dharma practice or any other activity. As we develop in the practice, we find that we make far fewer mistakes.

Another benefit is that because the mind is more peaceful and happy, we are a lot easier to get along with. We do not get as angry or act as petty as we used to, which not only makes us happy but other people as well. We are easy to be around, easy to live and work with, and easy to be married to.

Another benefit is that we become trustworthy. We are not so wild and unpredictable anymore; we are much more stable psychologically, which means that it is easier for people to know what we are going to do. As a result, we become reliable, and people start to have more confidence in us. This happens because one of shamata's functions is to weaken the kleshas.

We could say that the difference between a shamata practitioner and a non-practitioner is the difference between a cube-shaped block and a round ball. That is to say, someone who practices shamata cannot be rolled around that easily. When you develop a stable shamata practice, your mind stays where you put it; you are not at the mercy of every little change in your environment, not buffeted about by the slightest thing. Someone who does not possess this tranquility is like the ball, which has no ability to stay put. The slightest touch will roll it in whatever direction it is pushed. Normally, very slight changes in conditions or environment make people agitated because a little change produces a thought which snowballs into a state of agitation. Such people are not able to do anything effectively from a dharmic point of view, or even from a mundane point of view. Shamata, however, cuts through that.

Therefore, you need to continue to practice shamata until your mind is totally stabilized, because if you discard the practice simply on the basis of an ephemeral experience of tranquility, that feeling will quickly disappear and your previous state of instability will rise up again. You will be in exactly the same position as you were before you began the practice. Thus it is important to keep going with shamata practice, and it is also important to do it regularly. It is a little like eating: if you do not eat regularly, your body starts to waste away, and you may even die. It is the same with shamata practice: there has to be a constant input of tranquility through the practice of formal sitting. This keeps your mind stable and feeds the gradual development of the state of tranquility.

When your shamata practice gets to the point where you can direct your attention one-pointedly to whatever virtuous object you wish, then the particular shamata practice of directing attention to the breath is not necessary. If your mind can be directed one-pointedly to whatever technique and practice you are doing, simply direct your attention to that. The sign that you are ready to undertake such a practice is that when you are performing the practice, you are not interrupted by thought. If you are unable to maintain the visualization or whatever your practice is, if you are constantly distracted, then you might have to go back to the breath. The point is that when you have attained basic stability through shamata practice, the development of that stability continues in whatever practice you are performing.

I can think of an actual incident which illustrates this point. I had a student who was in intensive retreat. When he started practicing tantric visualization practices, he found that although he could chant the liturgies that go with the practices, and he could understand it all just fine, he could not do the visualizations. His mind would not stay put. So I suggested he do three months of shamata practice. Now, his three months of shamata practice were a little bit different from most people's because he was meditating eighteen hours per day. In any case, he did that for three months, and at the end of that time he found he could do anything he wanted with his mind. He could maintain any visualization for any length of time, and since that time he has been able to acquire the qualities associated with those advanced practices. I think the practice became workable for him because of accomplishing the training of shamata.

QUESTIONS AND ANSWERS

STUDENT: You said earlier that after practicing shamata, one might receive the pointing-out instruction, and thereafter could develop further. Would you explain that further?

RINPOCHE: The ultimate wisdom and qualities that are present in spiritual awakening are already possessed by each and every one of us; this wisdom is in fact the very essence of our minds. Since these have always been present, they are called co-emergent wisdom. We have always had these qualities, and we always will have them. We also have kleshas and bad habits, and these prevent us from recognizing what we really are and what we really have. Therefore, the point of the path is to remove the obscurations that block our co-emergent wisdom. In order to do that, we have to strengthen ourselves and accumulate merit; we have to chip away at our obscurations, and that leads to a gradual recognition of these qualities. We also need shamata practice, of course, which enables us to implement these various techniques.

Through this accumulation of merit and wisdom and through this stable shamata, space opens up in your obscurations, and it becomes possible for a lama to point out this co-emergent wisdom in the same way he or she would point out someone in a crowd. In Tibetan, this is called *ngötrö*, which literally means introduction, in the sense of introducing one person to another. Now, it is not certain that at the time of receiving this transmission you will immediately and fully recognize co-emergent wisdom with one word or gesture. What does happen is that you gain the certainty that you really do possess this wisdom.

Recognizing co-emergent wisdom brings about the certainty that if you can transcend your kleshas and bad habits, then the fruition is possible. For example, say you want to travel to a foreign country. If you get a glimpse of the country beforehand, then you know that it is there, what it is like, and which direction to go. Then you would know that if you set out toward that country, you would actually get there. In the same way, the real function of this introduction is to give the idea of where you are going. It is the ultimate encouragement to travel the path of practice.

STUDENT: How does meditation on the four thoughts that turn the mind relate to the practice of shamata, and to more involved practices such as the ngöndro?

RINPOCHE: In my opinion, this is an individual matter. Even if someone is a beginner, it is possible that he or she could be completely certain about the benefits of Dharma practice, certain that Dharma practice leads to certain qualities and certain results, and certain of the defects of not practicing Dharma. In addition, that person may find that meditation and contemplation on the four thoughts that turn the mind encourages and deepens a sense of confidence and understanding in the practice. If he or she is able to rest the mind within the structure of these contemplations, then in my opinion it is fine to begin with these contemplations and then proceed to ngöndro practice. However, when people ask me if they can start ngöndro practice and if I teach ngöndro to beginners, I do not have a general rule because it really depends upon the needs of the specific practitioner.

For example, if someone does not really understand what Dharma is, what it is all about, what its point is, and if he or she thinks ideas such as the defects of samsara, impermanence, and especially karma are a lot of nonsense, and if the contemplation of these things does not generate any genuine sadness and renunciation but simply generates jadedness and disrespect for Dharma, then I think that individual should begin by practicing shamata. If someone who does not initially have any confidence in Dharma is willing to practice shamata properly, then that person's experience in shamata will lead to certainty about the need for practice. Therefore, I think it is different in each individual case.

STUDENT: In connection with the necessity of shamata practice before proceeding with the higher levels of practice, what is the purpose of beginners being given tantric empowerments? Are these simply blessings?

RINPOCHE: There are two types of empowerments, not in the sense that the rituals are different, but in the sense that there are two types of students receiving empowerments. We can call one type the blessing empowerment, and the other the ultimate or actual empowerment. When the person receiving an empowerment understands exactly what is going on, and when the qualities associated with the empowerment are really transmitted to that person, this is an ultimate or actual empowerment. On the other hand, a blessing empowerment is when someone receives the empowerment through faith, confidence in the teacher, and confidence in the process, such as when a certain object is touched to their head and they feel the blessing. The function of receiving a blessing is that it plants a seed for the future practice of whatever deity is associated with the empowerment, and plants a seed for the future liberation of the person who receives the blessing.

I think it is quite appropriate for beginners to receive empowerments from authentic teachers because receiving the blessing with real trust and faith creates a very strong connection between student and teacher. In the future it will eventually ripen into that person's enlightenment, so it is really beneficial. However, it is not good to take an empowerment one day and then the next day to generate a negative view about the teacher. You must avoid that situation at all costs. So before you take an empowerment, you should make sure that you are going to continue to have confidence and faith in the teacher. There is no problem with receiving empowerments from different teachers, provided you understand that in essence all teachers are the same. This means having a continuing practice with a teacher, and viewing your other teachers as having the same nature as your original teacher. Then there is no problem.

The Ethical
Foundations of Practice

A s we have seen, shamata meditation leads to stillness of mind, and promotes the uncovering of our inherent wisdom. Sitting practice alone is not sufficient, however, for our development in the path. We need to put our clarity and wisdom into action in all of our life activities. In many ways the mindfulness developed in meditation practice is the natural basis for genuine ethical behavior, since what we do becomes less under the power of habits and rationalizations, and we have the spaciousness to reflect on the outcome of our actions. Therefore it has been said that shamata practice is the necessary companion to the practice of virtue.

The beginning point of the ethical teachings of Buddhism is the description of the ten negative and positive actions. These are presented as a general framework, one that points out what types of actions cause suffering and the perpetuation of confusion for ourselves and others, and what sorts of actions bring about happiness and wellbeing, and enable our progress toward wisdom.

These teachings are not presented as rules, although there are vows that you can take that are connected with them. What is important as a starting point, however, is to understand why some actions are negative and some positive, and to have the mindfulness and awareness to pursue a positive direction in our own lives. In particular, we need to recognize that our actions create what is called a karmic accumulation, which will affect our state of mind and our very life circumstances for better or worse in the future.

THE TEN NEGATIVE ACTIONS OF BODY, SPEECH, AND MIND

Traditionally, it is taught that there are ten negative actions of body, speech, and mind: three of body, four of speech, and three of mind. The body, speech, and mind are the source of all negative activities, with mind being the most powerful. Each of these negative actions can come about in association with the mental afflictions of attachment, aggression, and ignorance, and I will give examples of these connections along the way.

THE THREE NEGATIVE ACTIONS OF BODY

There are three negative actions of the body: killing, stealing, and sexual misconduct.

First we will discuss killing. I will explain this in connection with the three main types of mental afflictions: attachment, anger, and ignorance. The first is killing with attachment. An example of this would be killing an animal out of desire for the animal's meat, bones, skin, or fur. The second is killing with anger. We become angry and feel hatred, and therefore destroy another person or being. Third is killing out of ignorance. For example, some people enjoy taking life as a sport or form of entertainment and they are indifferent to the suffering they cause.

The second negative action of the body is stealing. Stealing refers to taking something that does not belong to you. Of course, if something is shared property, or if you have permission to take or use it, that is not regarded as stealing.

There are three categories of stealing, also connected with the three emotions of attachment, anger, and ignorance. We steal out of attachment because we see something attractive or valuable. Perhaps we are poor and cannot afford such an object, and so we steal it. Stealing out of anger means to steal something in order to cause suffering to the owner. It may not be of any help to the thief at all, but he or she takes it knowing that the other person will suffer from not having it. An example of stealing through ignorance would be when someone steals and harms another person without really needing the object or knowing that it was important to the owner. For example, you may take a small part of a machine, like a screw, not knowing that it will cause problems to the owner.

The third negative action of the body is sexual misconduct. Sexual misconduct refers to any use of sexuality that causes harm. Examples include rape, incest, having sexual relations with someone who is underage, having sexual relations with someone who has taken vows not to engage in sexual activity, or having sexual relations with someone who is married or in a committed relationship.

Sexual misconduct committed out of attachment means that someone is very attracted to another person. Even though one knows that the person is unavailable in some way such as being married or underage, there is such temptation, passion, and attachment, that one goes ahead and has sexual relations with them. Sexual misconduct committed out of anger might arise when someone wants to harm a couple or separate them. In order to create a division between them, he or she engages with one of them in a sexual way, therefore creating tremendous pain and difficulties. As well, needless to say, sexual activity without consent, such as the case of rape, is regarded as primarily an expression of aggression. Engaging in sexual misconduct out of ignorance comes about from being confused or unaware about one's partner. For example, the partner may be married, underage, or have taken vows of celibacy. Not knowing these facts about the real situation, one only finds out later that that it was sexual misconduct.

THE FOUR NEGATIVE ACTIONS OF SPEECH

The four negative actions of speech are lying, creating disharmony, harmful words, and gossip. As with the negative actions of the body, the negative actions of speech are connected to the three mental afflictions. For example, if you are very attached to something, you may lie to obtain whatever you are attached to. Lying out of anger means deceiving someone knowing that the person will suffer as a result of the lie. Lying out of ignorance means to lie based upon a lack of knowledge. For example, you may be asked directions to a particular location but give a wrong answer out of ignorance. Instead of saying, "I don't know," you give the wrong directions.

The second negative action of speech is to create disharmony among those who are harmonious. This could happen within a community, between a harmonious couple, or within a family. Disharmony can be created out of attachment, as might happen if someone is attached to having certain people as friends, and tries to create division within a group in hopes of obtaining these friends. By telling lies and saying things that create misconceptions, he or she tries to get "in" with a certain group by alienating them from their other friends. The second, creating disharmony out of anger, is obvious. The third, creating disharmony out of ignorance, can come about by saying something hurtful in a careless way. For example, we may thoughtlessly repeat something we have heard from someone else, creating disharmony within a group or between a couple.

The third negative action of speech is harsh words. Someone may say harsh words out of attachment in order to subdue others and dominate them. This was perhaps more common in ancient times when kings and ministers who were attached to their positions spoke harshly out of their desire to retain power. It is not necessary to say much about harsh words spoken in anger. We are all familiar with how people speak cruelly when they get angry and hurt others. An example of harsh words spoken out of ignorance would be various kinds of crude humor, such as racial or sexist jokes. The person telling the joke might just be trying to be funny, but it is still very offensive and hurtful.

The fourth negative action of speech is gossip. The Tibetan word for this is actually a slang expression similar to the English term "chit-chat." Gossip is one of the main ways we waste our lives. For example, suppose there are three people: one is a practitioner, one is a worker, and one is a gossip. While the practitioner is practicing and the worker is working, the gossip is chitchatting. After three hours, the practitioner has completed his practice, the worker has completed all or some of his work, but the person who was gossiping achieved neither the practice nor the work. Instead, that person's mind is filled with neurotic thought patterns, endless judgments, and speculation about the past and future. He or she has not achieved anything meaningful.

As before, gossip is connected to each of the three emotions. Attachment is simple: some people are just very attached to talking without any real purpose. They enjoy talking about the affairs of other people as well as their own lives, their past, and what they want to do in the future. They enjoy repeating these things over and over and over again. Gossip out of anger means to get satisfaction out of talking about the pain that others such as ex-lovers, parents, and so forth have caused. People tend to talk about these things over and over, but it really has no outcome. Of course it is sometimes necessary to talk about your experiences, but engaging in such gossip repeatedly is a waste of time. An example of the third case, engaging in gossip out of ignorance, is when someone pours out every sort of personal matter to people he or she barely knows, and without any real purpose. Such a person would talk about just about anything, not knowing what is appropriate or not, including subjects that would usually be kept private, such as sexual matters, fantasies, and fears. It is like opening a can and pouring out all the contents.*

THE THREE NEGATIVE ACTIONS OF MIND

The three negative actions of mind are envy, ill-will, and wrong view. Envy means not being able to appreciate what we have and being filled with desire for what others have. An envious person does not work to get what he or she desires, but simply covets the possessions or situations of others. This is related to the mental affliction of jealousy.

---

* Editor's note: What we often call gossip, as in negative talk that harms a person's reputation, would probably be considered divisive speech in this presentation of the ten negative actions.

The second is ill-will or harmful thoughts. Some people wish for others to suffer, and actually take delight in seeing other people's pain and misfortune. Such thoughts are not only destructive, but they prevent us from helping others. Harmful thoughts are obviously related to anger and aggression, but can also arise from jealousy and attachment.

The third is wrong view. Wrong view out of attachment is, for example, being so attached to a certain view as to not be willing to give it up, even if it is clearly harmful. The denial of alcoholics and drug addicts is a good example of this. Their actions are dangerous to their health and all those around them. They have become attached to a particular substance, and because they are not ready to give it up, they find excuses. Wrong view out of anger is a situation where someone intentionally tries to make wrong that which is right, with the intention of harming others. Wrong view out of ignorance means that someone is confused and does not know what is right and what is wrong.

Some people may think, "If I do not engage in these negative actions of body, speech, and mind, people will think I am not normal, and I will be so different that I will never have any friends." If you look at this with a more practical mind, you will see that most wise people respect a person who is honest and truthful, and they also appreciate a person who has a soft, gentle nature. Nobody really enjoys harsh words. In the case of gossip, you might find some friends who like that, but honestly, wise people do not really like gossip. As for stealing, almost everyone would prefer to be friends with someone who does not steal, simply because that person can be trusted. There may be some communities where the members steal, tell lies, and so forth, and you may not be welcomed by these groups because you will not be suited to such people. However, in most social groups, if you practice Dharma and avoid the ten negative actions of body, speech, and mind, you will be genuinely respected.

With respect to the relative effects of the different types of negative actions, the least amount of negative karma is created by negative actions performed out of ignorance. A somewhat more negative result comes from negative actions that have been committed out of attachment. However, the most powerful negative result occurs from actions that are connected with anger or hatred.

You may wonder why it is important to know about these ten negative actions. It is important because we all have the three mental afflictions of attachment, anger, and ignorance. As long as we have these emotions, we will constantly be drawn towards one or another of the ten negative actions. Some of us were fortunate to have the kind of upbringing in which we were taught not to encourage or give power to these mental afflictions. That is not the case for everyone, of course, and in any case, as long as we are under the power of the negative emotions, we will repeatedly engage in negative actions of body, speech, and mind out of our attachment, anger, and ignorance. The knowledge that these actions are negative, and their psychological source, is a first step to disengaging from such activities.

In the next section, we will explore the corresponding ten positive actions, and how to work with and overcome the mental afflictions. We will see that in order to pacify the three mental afflictions of attachment, anger, and ignorance, we must first learn to develop the qualities of calm abiding through sitting meditation. Once we have pacified these patterns on the foundation of shamata meditation, we then apply insight meditation, which totally uproots the three mental afflictions. This brings freedom from the causes of the ten negative actions of body, speech, and mind.

If you do not address this problem at its root, it is very hard to avoid negative actions. For example, suppose you want to get rid of a huge tree that has thousands of branches. If you were to cut each branch individually, it would take months to complete your work. Even if you cut it completely down to the root, new branches will grow back eventually. In this case, the practical thing to do is to uproot the tree.

In the same way, the effective way to get rid of negative actions of body, speech, and mind is to uproot the disturbing emotions, which are the root of these negative activities. To do this, you should first pacify your mind by means of shamata meditation, developing calmness and stillness. With this preparation, you should then apply vipasyana to totally burn up or uproot the mental afflictions.

QUESTIONS AND ANSWERS

STUDENT: I have a question about speech. It seems very difficult not to participate in non-virtuous actions of speech, especially at work, where it is very difficult to avoid divisive talk. An example might be if someone is attempting to do a big project. One person is using a certain kind of software and somebody else is using another. This is all right when they work alone, but if they have to put a project together, it won't work. So I have to tell these two people, "Hey, you are not doing things right." In this way, I could end up turning what was a peaceful situation into one where people disagree with each other. So it seems hard to balance non-divisive speech with getting the job done. Is it better to keep quiet in situations like that?

RINPOCHE: No. Speech can be either positive or negative. If you see a mistake being made in some project, there is no reason for you to remain silent. However, before you speak, it is important to analyze very carefully whether there is a selfish reason behind pointing out the fault. If there is no selfish purpose but you are really just seeing a mistake—some problem with the project such that the work will not be completed—then that is not negative speech at all. It *is* negative, however, when there is a selfish purpose, such as pointing out errors to make yourself look good or feel important.

STUDENT: In the summertime, insects and mice get into my house. I do not like to have them there, but what do I do? Do I kill them?

RINPOCHE: This is a very difficult subject to discuss. As you gradually train your mind, you develop a sense of understanding about the equality of humans, animals, and insects. In the sense that the world belongs to everybody, it is necessary to learn to share. However, until you have properly trained your mind, that openness does not exist, and you will see things in terms of "my territory, his territory."

On the one hand, if you decide it is all right to kill anything that gets in your territory, you might take the lives of thousands of insects or hundreds of mice. Therefore it would not be proper to give you the go-ahead to take life. At the same time, if I say that you should not kill at all, that could be very difficult, because these creatures can create serious problems for yourself and others. All I can say is that if we commit ourselves in the present to train our minds, this will help us realize how to skillfully handle such situations in the future.

STUDENT: Could you discuss how we can incorporate mindfulness practice into our everyday lives?

RINPOCHE: The way we incorporate the mindfulness of meditation into our daily life is very similar to how we begin to learn to read and write. At the beginning, it is quite difficult to remember the alphabet. The reason we eventually learned the alphabet is because our teachers repeatedly taught it to us, using various techniques until we became accustomed to the signs and structure. Later, when we began to write, we did not have to think about how to write the letter "A"; it just flowed naturally because we had become accustomed to it.

Similarly, if you make it a habit of meditating every day, even if only for a very short period of time, you will build up within yourself a familiarization with meditation. You can then carry the energy of that familiarization throughout your life whether you are working, speaking with people, or just taking a walk. That sort of energy remains within you.

It is like eating food. When you are hungry you eat, and then you are satisfied. You are not hungry every hour, but you are able to maintain that satisfaction for a certain number of hours because of the energy of the food. Similarly, the energy of meditation is such that it stays with you, and this helps you incorporate it into your life.

However, if you do not maintain the consistency of meditation, the energy of meditation will deteriorate. If there is no consistent meditation to energize you, you will completely lose mindfulness in your daily life. Therefore consistency is the main thing.

STUDENT: I was interested in what you said about chit-chat, that we lose time and do not accomplish any dharma activities. For me, chit-chat can be a vehicle for finding out about other people. Even for purposes of the dharma, it is not so easy to be completely direct, and I can find out a lot of things by nonchalantly talking to people. So, is it the motivation that makes speech chit-chat? If it doesn't stop me from accomplishing my duties, is chit-chat entirely negative?

RINPOCHE: You are right that many positive things can come from discussion. Probably the Tibetan term *ngag kyal* and the English word "gossip" do not convey exactly the same meaning. Ngag kyal means to talk about a meaningless subject, so what is considered a negative action is talk that has no purpose.

If from today onward you carefully examine the speech of others, you will find that some people talk with no purpose, but are simply dwelling upon good things they experienced in the past. There is no achievement or purpose to their talk because while they are talking about the past, they miss the present. If you miss something you had in the past that you do not have now, there is no point talking about it.

People get so carried away by gossip. When they are washing the dishes, they pick up a few plates and suddenly start gossiping to each other. They could spend two hours holding the plates in their hands, just talking and not doing any washing. What did they achieve with this talk? Nothing. Talk like that is gossip because it has no purpose. Discussion is something that has some point, some meaning. If you are planning a project, that kind of talk is a discussion, not chit-chat or gossip.

STUDENT: You have spoken about cause and effect, and how our actions cause certain effects. Could you say more about the cause and effect that has to do with happiness and suffering, virtue and non-virtue?

RINPOCHE: In general, with respect to cause and effect, if you cultivate negative things, you experience negative things. This does not mean that if you cause others pain, you will have the exact same experience with the exact same kind of pain. The meaning of cause and effect is that because you caused pain for others, you then have to experience pain, but it is not definite how you will experience it. The pain is more of a general outcome that will inevitably result.

For example, suppose you had done something in a past life that caused suffering and pain for others, and suppose in this life you become very ill. The illness is not the same as the pain you caused in the past, but your illness is the effect.

It is also possible for people to experience collective suffering due to shared karma. For example, if someone makes a bomb and drops it, causing suffering for many. You may ask, "Why do all these people experience suffering at the same time? What sort of karma could there be that they would experience suffering at the same time, from one bomb?" Well, we are always accumulating shared negative karma. Such shared karma is the reason there is shared suffering.

STUDENT: Sometimes I wonder if every instance of harsh speech is negative. Sometimes I feel that the only way I can relate to someone who is doing something harmful is to be rough. Could it be possible to use harsh speech with the proper motivation? Do we always have to work things out in a soft way?

RINPOCHE: The harsh words that I discussed earlier are those based upon the emotion of anger, which often leads to hatred. With this mixture of mental afflictions, it is a negative action to use any sort of harsh words. This is because when there is hatred involved, your mind is filled with the wish to destroy another person.

There can also be harsh words spoken with positive intentions. This is more in the sense of being wrathful, as parents sometime speak to children or teachers to students. We speak in this way in order to create something positive for others, for example, to help them develop discipline. Hatred is not involved in this; the harsh words are used without any negative intention. I have said many times that we cannot always discipline others with peaceful means. We have to show wrath sometimes, but underneath there is no hatred.

Those who are not clear about this wrath without hate should study the life story of the great yogi Milarepa (1040-1123 C.E.).[2] When Milarepa was a student, his teacher Marpa[3] constantly used harsh words and beat him. His intention was to discipline and teach him, and because of that Milarepa obtained enlightenment in one lifetime. The mind of Marpa was pure and free from hate, yet he showed wrathfulness in order to discipline Milarepa. This is the more positive sense of being harsh.

STUDENT: Could you explain again how basic ignorance leads to mental afflictions?

RINPOCHE: Ignorance is the basic source of the ten negative actions of body, speech, and mind because it involves not knowing or understanding that these activities are negative. Not knowing right from wrong, proper from improper, believing what we think is correct and not being open to a deeper understanding of right and wrong, we constantly indulge in the ten negative actions.

STUDENT: With respect to ignorance and wrong view, ignorance is one of the three mental afflictions. Ignorance and wrong view seem to be very similar, yet they must be different. Do they go hand in hand? Which comes first?

RINPOCHE: Actually, fundamental ignorance is the source or basis of the ten negative actions of body, speech, and mind. In the case of wrong view, we are involved with, or endorse, so to speak, the fundamental ignorance, and the wrong view arises from that. Because of ignorance, we do not know what is right and what is wrong, and so we believe in what is wrong because we think it is right. Wrong view means to strongly support a wrong idea, to participate further in the ignorance. This comes from and is influenced by ignorance.

---

2   The great Tibetan yogi saint.
3   The founder of the Kagyu lineage, Marpa (1012-1097 C.E.) was renowned for bringing back tantric texts from India.

The Ten Positive Actions of Body, Speech, and Mind

THE ETHICAL FOUNDATIONS OF PRACTICE

W e have discussed how the ten negative actions relate to the three doors of body, speech, and mind. Similarly, the ten positive actions also spring from these three doors.

It helps to know about negative actions because we often wonder, "Why can't I get along with my family? Why can't I succeed like so and so?" By knowing about the ten negative actions, we can gain insight without needing to find someone to blame for our own failures, insecurities, and weaknesses. We understand that we undergo tremendous pain and misfortune due to having engaged in negative actions of body, speech, and mind. Not only do we come to understand this, but we learn to take more responsibility for our actions, learning how to protect ourselves and do better for ourselves, and eventually learning how to be of greater benefit to others. Knowledge of our negative actions does help answer many of the questions we have been asking, and helps us take greater responsibility for ourselves in the future. Once we understand the negative actions, we can go on to understand and practice the corresponding positive actions. As we'll see, they don't merely consist of avoiding the negative actions, although they are in some sense mirror images of each other.

THE THREE POSITIVE ACTIONS OF BODY

The first negative action of body is killing. Conversely, the first positive action of body is not only refraining from killing, but protecting life as well. Killing leads to the experience of suffering in the future, whereas not killing preserves the fundamental virtue in our lives. But protecting life, we deepen our positive karmic accumulation, which energizes our strength of virtue.

In our society, there are many groups of people who protect animal rights, which I strongly support. They are protecting lives, which is very virtuous. Apart from saying that it is virtuous not to take the lives of other beings, what are the karmic benefits of not killing? If we take the lives of others, our lives will be threatened by many obstacles, and we will not enjoy long life. Conversely, if we do not kill and instead protect life, we will enjoy the benefits of a long, healthy life.

Some people experience very long lives, but they are constantly ill. If we always get sick even though we take good care of ourselves, these illnesses could be the result of the karma from our past lives. We may not have taken lives, but we somehow enjoyed, participated in, or indulged in harming beings. As a result of these actions, even if you have a long life your health will be plagued by various illnesses.

The second negative action of body is stealing, and the opposite of that, the positive action, is not stealing. We could also look at this in terms of cause and effect, the negative karma that someone acquires because of stealing. Sometimes people wonder why a child might take birth in a country that is extremely poor and hot, a place where all the people are starving. The answer is that the child did not choose starvation or the place and time of his or her birth; rather, because of negative karma accumulated through stealing, the child took rebirth in such a place of extreme poverty.

The opposite of stealing is, of course, not stealing. Again, in order to energize this virtue and make the benefit greater, you should not only avoid stealing, but you should try to be generous and open. As a result of such virtuous activity, you take birth within a loving, caring family in a prosperous country. Not only that, but as you mature your career and everything you need in order to achieve your goals goes well. This happens effortlessly because of the strength of the positive karma of generosity; this is how cause and effect work. However, if you have not cultivated the seed, there will be no fruit, regardless which deities you ask for blessings. The seed of positive karma is virtue, particularly the virtue of generosity, and the outcome of this generosity is your own well-being, success, and prosperity.

The Buddhist deity Dzambhala is known as the deity of wealth and prosperity. The idea that there could be a deity of wealth and prosperity in Buddhism intrigues many Westerners. The moment students hear teachings from lamas about the deity of wealth, they say, "I want to practice that deity! I want to become rich immediately!" Such students make a serious attempt to do the practice of the deity of wealth, but if they have not cultivated virtuous seeds in the past, the deity of wealth will not be able to help them.

There is a story that illustrates this point. In ancient times there was a poor beggar whose only means of survival was traveling from place to place asking for food. Somehow he received the complete practice and empowerment of Dzambhala, the deity of wealth. He practiced it so much that one day he actually saw Dzambhala right in front of him. Dzambhala said, "Why have you been calling me all this time?" The beggar replied, "I need wealth. I need prosperity." Dzambhala disappeared, but he appeared on another day and said, "Go to this particular monastery today and you will receive a special blessing."

The beggar was very excited, and he went to the monastery. He saw many beggars at the gates putting out their bowls and getting soup. The beggar had his bowl filled, and he saw that his soup had a small piece of meat in it. After he ate the food he thought to himself, "I didn't get anything special! What if the deity of wealth was lying to me?" He went home very disappointed, and practiced until Dzambhala appeared again. The beggar said to him, "You liar! I went all the way there and received nothing special." Dzambhala smiled and told him, "The rest of the beggars did not have meat. You got a piece of meat; that was only for you."

Dzambhala explained that because the beggar had not accumulated any positive karma in the past, there was no source from which he could be given anything positive. Long ago, he once gave a little food to a starving person, and because of that generosity, the deity of wealth was able to provide him with a piece of meat. The point is, if we want to be successful and experience good health and virtuous outcomes, we should not just look up to the deities and say, "Please give me success and wealth." We ourselves have to accomplish positive actions.

The third negative action of the body is sexual misconduct. The negative karmic effects of sexual misconduct within this lifetime are that you will experience pain, misery, and suffering. However, with respect to the next birth and future births, sexual misconduct in this life will lead you to take rebirth in an impure environment, and in addition, you will have bad health and be physically ugly. Therefore, the pain and suffering resulting from that misconduct will extend beyond this present life.

Those who have consistently engaged in sexual misconduct in a past life will find it difficult to find a partner, regardless how much they try. They might think it is a matter of personality or upbringing. However, the problem is actually a result of accumulated negative karma. This energy is so powerful that people naturally, without any superficial reason, do not want to be close to such a person.

The opposite of sexual misconduct is proper conduct, respecting other people's vows and wishes, and being committed to your own vows or a particular partner. Being committed in this way or being content with a single partner creates positive karma. Not only will you have some feeling of security and well-being in this life, but the next birth will be in a healthy, beautiful environment. Because of the natural energy that has accumulated due to your positive karma, you will be gracious, attractive, and surrounded by good friends.

Sometimes people say that our physical appearance is based upon the way our parents look, but even good looking parents have unattractive children. Therefore the appearance of the parents does not entirely explain the appearance of their children. People also think that if parents are virtuous the child will likewise be good, but that is also not always the case. A child could be totally different psychologically from his or her parents, and sometimes look and seem quite different from them as well. This is a result of karma.

THE FOUR POSITIVE ACTIONS OF SPEECH

The second category of positive actions is virtuous actions of speech. The first negative action of speech is to lie, and the opposite of lying is to not lie, to be truthful. If you are honest and truthful, the karmic result is that you will not only be trusted in this particular lifetime, but you will not be deceived by others in the next lifetime or for many lifetimes to come. In addition, your speech will be valued and respected by others.

The second negative action of speech is to create disharmony. When you create disharmony among a group of friends, you do not bring yourself or the others any peace or happiness. The opposite of this is the positive action of not creating disharmony. This includes not only not creating disharmony, but the act of trying to bring people together who have experienced division or separation. Having created harmony among people through skillful means, you will be surrounded by trustworthy friends. Such people are hard to find; there are always friends, but finding trustworthy people is a different matter. Also, in the next life you will be able to continue benefiting others through creating harmony because the energy of your actions stays with you.

The third negative action of speech is harsh words. If you are harsh to people, you will experience the result of that in this life and the next. You will receive a lot of criticism and be degraded by people; you will lack friends, and even if you think that a person is your friend, you discover they are criticizing you behind your back. You will not experience any sense of happiness or relief, but constantly feel criticism from family, friends, and others. This not only disturbs your peace of mind, but is very painful to live with.

The positive action of speech which is the opposite of harsh words is gentle speech. Harsh words come out of hatred or anger; you become angry and then say harsh words that hurt. Instead, you should try not to react immediately and be more sensible and cautious, and in this way maintain a sense of mindfulness of being gentle. As a result of the positive karma of gentle speech, in the next birth you will have an extremely melodious voice. You could become a great singer, and perhaps you will become quite well-known for your beautiful voice. In addition to having such an attractive voice, you will also be praised by people and not be subject to much criticism.

The fourth negative action of speech is gossip. We have a general idea of how we waste time by indulging in gossip, rumors, and so forth. The example given was to waste time talking about senseless, meaningless things, and thereby not achieving anything spiritually or materially.

The result of indulging in gossip is that we lose people's trust. The more we talk about meaningless things, the less people like to spend time with us because they hate to listen to that kind of talk. We are not aware of repeating things over and over because we think we are making some great point, but the listener is very aware that we have repeated something several times, and they are tired of it. Perhaps the person will be polite and not say anything, but the next time they will try to avoid us. This is how talking about meaningless things might make us lose friends. As well, due to the habitual pattern of enjoying gossip, we do not accomplish much by way of spiritual practice, nor do we achieve our worldly goals. We can carry this strong habitual pattern into the next lifetime as well.

In contrast to this, the fourth positive action of speech is saying meaningful things about meaningful subjects. As well, whatever you talk about, you speak with a sense of gentleness. Using your skill, intelligence, and common sense, you are careful that whatever you say will not harm anyone. It is very important to be sure of this before we speak. If we speak with gentleness on all subjects, this will help everyone learn something new, and people will like to be with us and talk to us because we make sense. Anyone would want to talk to a person who makes sense and does not waste their time.

THE THREE POSITIVE ACTIONS OF MIND

The first negative action of mind is envy. It means desiring something that someone else has. Someone who is envious is always fantasizing about something impossible. Since it is a quality of the mind, the attitude of envy is actually limitless. No doubt, for example, someone could think, "I wish that I possessed the whole United States of America." Of course, it is impossible for one person to possess the entire United States. However, because this mind of envy is so powerful and so gross, no room is left to consider anyone else. They would not even think, "I wish that I possessed half of America, and other people could possess the other half." They want to possess the entire country. The negative karma of such an envious mind is very powerful.

The opposite of envy is the first virtuous action of mind, generosity. To be envious means to be selfish, wanting everything you see for yourself. Because of this envy, the ability to give freely becomes impossible. It is in this sense that the opposite of envy is generosity, which results in positive karma.

Comparatively speaking, the United States is very well-developed and the people are quite well-off, so not everyone in this country is under the power of envy. In other parts of the world, however, I have encountered many people who are. They want to have everything they see, always thinking, "I wish this were mine." Envious thoughts are thoughts of constantly wishing to possess something, and there is nothing positive about thinking in this way.

The second negative action of mind is ill-will. It means having harmful thoughts. A person who enjoys and feeds these kinds of thoughts would be someone who thinks about and is entertained by the suffering of others.

The opposite of harmful thoughts are altruistic thoughts. In their fully developed form, altruistic thoughts are known as enlightened mind or bodhicitta. Enlightened mind not only benefits ourselves, but is the source of energy that provides happiness for others. It is the source of all happiness and virtue, as well as many other positive qualities.

The third negative action of mind is wrong view. As we have defined it, wrong view is based upon a deluded mind, not knowing wrong to be wrong and right to be right. We mistakenly take that which is wrong to be right, and that which is right to be wrong. Then we develop a strong fixation on that mistake, such that even when someone else tries to explain our error, we are unwilling to accept their explanation. We simply go on believing what we did before; we hold on to our wrong view without being willing to explore further. Having a wrong view means that we have closed the door to anything positive, and thus there is no source of positive qualities available to us.

The opposite of wrong view is very simple. By opening the door to understanding and learning, we are able to eliminate the mistake of confusing what is wrong with what is right. Being able and willing to learn is the positive quality. In the absence of wrong view, our insight is naturally developed, and this becomes a source of virtue.

WORKING WITH MENTAL AFFLICTIONS

An essential part of the Buddhist path is to learning how to deal with the kleshas, which is the Sanskrit term for mental afflictions. There are three stages to uprooting our kleshas: first, recognizing our mental afflictions; second, considering the defects that result from being under the power of mental afflictions; and finally, engaging in whatever methods are necessary to abandon and transcend the power of mental afflictions.

In the Tibetan tradition, the methods of practice are presented in terms of the lesser vehicle, the greater vehicle, and the highest vehicle. The Sanskrit terms for these three are hinayana, mahayana, and vajrayana. We will examine methods for working with mental afflictions according to the hinayana and mahayana. We will not discuss the vajrayana in this book in any detail because those concepts and practices are rather advanced. You can, however, receive teachings on this subject once you get to advanced stages of practice.

RECOGNIZING MENTAL AFFLICTIONS

Mental afflictions are continually present in all of our minds. They are the essential cause of our suffering, and they destroy our attempts to find happiness. However, the kleshas are not inherent to the nature of our minds; if they were, it would not be possible to abandon or transcend them. The trouble is that we fail to recognize kleshas as problematic, and we fail to recognize the effect they have on the way we experience the world.

Even though the kleshas are the cause of our suffering, we generally mistake them for positive qualities, things we would like to cultivate and enhance. But as long as we try to increase them, we will never really be happy. It is similar to someone mistaking poison for medicine: a person feels ill, and then they drink a bottle of poison hoping to remove the illness. The poison does not help, and it also creates additional problems.

The mental afflictions are traditionally often called the three poisons. The word poison is a metaphor for suffering, the feeling of poisoned experience. The three poisons are attachment, aversion, and ignorance. The root of all mental afflictions, however, is ignorance. It is through the presence of ignorance that mental afflictions arise, and it is through the presence of ignorance that they increase in power. In the same way, the removal of ignorance causes a corresponding lessening of the power of mental afflictions.

The presence of mental afflictions leads to a limitless variety of problems and suffering. If we look carefully at the situations we experience, we can see that all the fear, danger, and terror that we undergo, as well as the actual suffering and adverse conditions, arise from the presence of mental afflictions. This occurs because the mental afflictions cause a person under their power to engage in afflicted action, which creates an imprint in that person's mind. The result of the imprint of these actions is the experience of future suffering. Since this is the way events transpire, we can say that the root of all suffering and evil in the world is due to people being under the power of mental afflictions.

Unfortunately, what usually happens is that when we undergo different kinds of problems and fears, when we experience different kinds of suffering and danger, rather than recognizing that these are produced by mental afflictions, we believe they are caused by the specific external conditions that irritate or threaten us. On the basis of that belief, we generate further aversion and mental affliction, which compounds our suffering. This process gains momentum and keeps getting stronger, and as long as it continues we will not experience any genuine happiness in all our future lifetimes.

This is not merely something that affects us in this lifetime; this has been going on throughout a period of time that in fact has no beginning. We can say that mental affliction is our primordial enemy.

The mental afflictions are our genuine enemy. Normally when we say "enemy" we refer to someone who does something to us that we do not like. But the worst thing a conventional enemy can do is steal everything we have or kill us. Yet once this enemy kills us, their power is finished; he or she cannot harm us continually over an endless period of time. Mental afflictions, on the other hand, have been tormenting us continually during a time that has no beginning and will continue to do so until we do something about them.

Again, with conventional enemies, there may be a way to soften them up a bit. We might be able to befriend them, and in fact we know that enemies often do become our friends. And even if we cannot make friends with our enemies in this life, they may be our friend in a future life, so there is nothing permanent or substantial about the relationship. However, no matter how hard we try to befriend mental afflictions—and we try to do this all the time—it never works. They never soften up, and they never stop tormenting us. If you think about the actual harm caused by mental afflictions, you will come to understand why it is necessary to do whatever you can to transcend their influence and get rid of them.

TAMING MENTAL AFFLICTIONS:
The Approach of the Hinayana

Once we recognize the harm that comes from mental afflictions, it is time to start taming them. The methods for doing this are set forth in the many teachings of the Dharma that the Buddha gave us. The reason there are many different approaches to dealing with the kleshas is so we can accord with individual practitioners' different levels of ability and diligence.

The approach of hinayana is also called the "common vehicle" since it is common to all the other vehicles. From the point of view of the common vehicle, the basic level of practice, you begin by seeing the defects of mental afflictions. Then you can gradually extricate yourself from their control, principally by applying great care in the conduct of body and speech. This approach is similar to the approach you might take with a volatile enemy toward whom you would go to great lengths to avoid antagonizing. In the same way, you take great care with your body and speech so as not to antagonize or inflame your own mental afflictions.

In this the approach, therefore, you renounce everything that could possibly inflame the mental afflictions. You become a homeless refugee, a renunciate, and you try not to make another home out of your renunciation. Probably you would live in some kind of solitude and not worry much about your food and clothing. This type of approach is like running from an enemy who frightens you terribly. It is an effective and appropriate approach because as we become free from the immediate harm of mental afflictions, we have time to gradually conquer them and prevent them from increasing their control over us. This approach is initially based upon the desire to accomplish your own liberation from their power, and to accomplish your own permanent peace and happiness.

TAMING MENTAL AFFLICTIONS:
The Approach of the Mahayana

The mahayana or greater vehicle approach to taming mental afflictions is distinguished by the application of extraordinary insight and skill. The insight consists of the recognition that mental afflictions are simply events that occur in your mind when certain conditions are present. They are not inherently existing things. When those conditions are present, then what we call a mental affliction arises. When the conditions cease to be present, the afflictions disappear as completely as if they were never there.

Shantideva said that as long as we do not apply the remedy to mental afflictions, they just keep on coming and never stop. But if we look directly at their nature, we find that they do not have any nature. They do not have any inherent characteristics and are entirely conditional, which means they are based upon what is happening around them. The mental afflictions are simply events that occur in our minds through our own power; they have no power of their own. They have no nature of their own which can afflict us unless we attempt to manipulate them. In the case of a conventional enemy, even if we disregard the enemy and stop fighting, the enemy still might attack. On the other hand, if we leave mental afflictions alone and give up trying to coerce or gain from them, they cannot do anything because they do not exist.

From the mahayana point of view, the problem is simply that we have failed to recognize that the events we call mental afflictions are entirely conditioned things that do not exist inherently. Or if we have recognized this, it is merely an intellectual realization that has not really penetrated how we experience the world. Therefore the mahayana approach is to see the true nature of mental afflictions and thereby transcend their power.

The other aspect of the greater vehicle approach to taming mental afflictions is skillfulness, which in this context refers to the development of compassion. When we recognize that mental afflictions have no nature of their own, the motivation that fuels this recognition and the attendant transcendence is the thought that we are not the only people who suffer from mental afflictions. In fact, all other beings have always suffered from the same things that we have always suffered from. When we recognize that all sentient beings suffer from the same cause, we develop compassion, courage, and increased strength. Before, we ran away from the mental afflictions, but now our compassion helps us to recognize our commonality with all beings, and we see right through the kleshas.

Thus the mahayana approach consists of the insight that the mental afflictions are simply conditioned things, and this insight is then integrated with skillfulness, which is the development and application of compassion. The combination of insight and motivation leads to a confidence that starts to ripen into delight and joy, qualities which cut through the pettiness of mental afflictions.

Since mental afflictions are the cause of all our problems, the taming of mental afflictions is really the only aim that exists for Buddhist practitioners. Because there is no other aim, there is nothing else to try to do in our practice; there is no other quality we are trying to obtain, nothing special aside from this attempt to tame our kleshas. Traditionally, it is said that the only real sign of genuine Dharma practice is the lessening of mental afflictions.

You may wonder what happens when we succeed in taming the mental afflictions, and what change occurs. What happens is that we start to become happy. There are two kinds of happiness that develop: short-term happiness and long-term happiness. If we are happy right now, it is because our kleshas are not present. If we do not have mental affliction right now, we cannot be unhappy because unhappiness consists of mental affliction. The reason we experience long-term happiness is that the cause of long-term unhappiness is the imprint of afflicted actions, and we only perform afflicted actions under the power of mental afflictions. The result of all this pacification and happiness is the accomplishment of our own ultimate benefit as well as the ultimate benefit of others.

Normally, when we refer to benefiting ourselves, most people think this means doing something selfish. But selfish actions are anything but beneficial to us. This is because what really benefits us is making ourselves happy, and the only way to do this is to tame our mental afflictions. However, what people usually think benefits themselves does anything but that. Selfish actions actually destroy any possibility of benefit because such actions deepen the mental afflictions and leave us ensnared by them. If we wish to practice the Dharma, we must begin by recognizing that the key is to tame the mental afflictions.

Shantideva said that although all beings wish to be happy, they run towards the causes of their own destruction and misery. Every one of us, without exception, wants one thing: to be happy. However, through ignorance we fail to recognize the causes of happiness and the causes of suffering, and so we attempt to accomplish happiness through the cultivation of attachment, aversion, and ignorance. Until we recognize that attachment, aversion, and ignorance are not the causes of happiness but the causes of suffering, our aims and our actions will continue to be contradictory. Therefore it is necessary to distinguish between genuine causes of happiness and genuine causes of suffering. If we have correct insight, whatever goodness we cultivate will remain genuine and true. Whether it is a little or a lot, we stay on track because we know what is truly going on.

The root of all Dharma in both the lesser and the greater vehicles is taming mental afflictions. This is what is common to all Dharma; there is really not any difference. The only difference between the lesser vehicle and the greater vehicle is the vastness of our scope and intention. If we are concerned primarily with our own liberation and our own freedom from suffering, this is the lesser vehicle; if our primary concern is to liberate all beings from the same suffering that we experience, this is the greater vehicle. They are the same, however, in recognizing that we have to transcend the power of mental afflictions.

QUESTIONS AND ANSWERS

STUDENT: How does one develop the insight that one needs to transcend mental afflictions in order to be happy?

RINPOCHE: Whatever approach is taken in order to relate to mental afflictions, there has to be some kind of insight. This insight is generated first through hearing, then through contemplation. Hearing refers first to the acquisition of information. For example, through hearing information about mental afflictions, we come to some kind of understanding. However, this understanding by itself is not sufficient because it is just something that wandered into our ears. We have to take it a step further and generate a definitive understanding by analyzing the information with all the intelligence we can bring to bear on the question. We do this until we arrive at a point where there is no doubt that we understand the entire issue. Then we have that insight.

STUDENT: When someone becomes full of anger or desire and at that moment recognizes, "Oh, I'm full or anger" or "I'm full of desire," what can he or she do about it?

RINPOCHE: The kind of recognition you are talking about could help a bit in the sense that when we recognize mental affliction, we can look at what is happening, how we feel, and see how unpleasant it is. That might lead to this general recognition, and it might slightly lessen the kleshas' power since we do not want to continue this state of misery. But from another point of view, it is already too late because the klesha has arisen. Therefore, it is best to prepare beforehand. We have to prepare beforehand by recognizing in a general way the defects of mental afflictions. Then, when we meet with the conditions that generate mental afflictions, whether it is anger, desire, or attachment, they will not arise in the same way, or they will arise with less power. It is a little like going on a journey, part of which will take you on a treacherous path through the mountains. Knowing what is ahead, you have to be prepared to be careful.

STUDENT: What is the original source of the kleshas? Why do human beings develop in such a way that they are ruled by kleshas?

RINPOCHE: The source of all mental afflictions is ignorance, but it is an ignorance that has no beginning. There was never a first moment of ignorance so we cannot say that it started somewhere. The function of this ignorance is to generate mental afflictions which cause us to engage in afflicted actions, or karma. The imprints of these actions generate further mental afflictions, as well as external conditions which will generate more mental afflictions and suffering. Therefore both the causes and results of suffering have been going on from a time that has no beginning, and are therefore called primordial or beginningless.

STUDENT: Is basic ignorance the belief that our unhappiness comes from external conditions and objects rather than internal events or causes that we ourselves create?

RINPOCHE: What we mean by ignorance is ignorance about one thing: the idea that we exist. Ignorance or confusion is defined as taking that which is not a self and has no inherent existence to be a self that possesses inherent existence. Because we see things in this bewildered and distorted way, mental afflictions and suffering arise.

STUDENT: So basic ignorance is that a self exists?

RINPOCHE: Yes.

STUDENT: Is it possible to ascertain the cause of afflictions without the application of insight? I'm thinking of therapies that are not insight-based.

RINPOCHE: I do not know. It is quite complicated because there has to be some kind of recognition of the real problem. Regardless of what the discipline is or how it presents itself, if there is a real recognition on the part of the participants, a real insight into where the problems come from, the problems can be solved. The concern is that you could take a superficial approach and just deal with temporary causes or symptoms. That would be like cleaning the surface of a table, just wiping a cloth across its surface. It would not really change anything.

STUDENT: Could you say a little bit more about the benefits of seeing mental afflictions as events that just happen?

RINPOCHE: The benefit of that insight is that mental afflictions will not arise. If and when they do arise, they will be self-liberated because you will have no fixation on them. Through seeing that they have no inherent existence, you will have no fixation, and fixation is the fuel of mental afflictions. At that point, mental affliction would be like something drawn in water: as it is drawn, it starts to disappear and there is nothing left behind. However, this is only the case if your insight is a genuine realization. This is quite different from a theoretical understanding, because when kleshas arise in actual situations, a theoretical understanding cannot help.

STUDENT: How do you define mindfulness, and is mindfulness the transcendence of mental afflictions? How does that relate to becoming enlightened?

RINPOCHE: The root meaning of the term for mindfulness in Tibetan is to remember, to not forget. There are different kinds of mindfulness: there could be a mindfulness of virtue, and there could be a sort of evil mindfulness as well. When we talk about mindfulness in the context of practice, we mean the momentum arising from our intention not to lose sight of what we are trying to do and what we are trying to avoid. This means not allowing ourselves to lose our cultivation of virtue and goodness, and not allowing ourselves to fall into the cultivation of that which is harmful. As for the relationship between mindfulness and the abandoning of mental afflictions, mindfulness is a method of abandoning them rather than the result of having abandoned them.

Concerning enlightenment or awakening, the Tibetan term for this is *jangchup*, and it has quite a deep meaning. The first syllable *jang* means purified or removed, and it means that all mental afflictions are gone for good and can never come back.

Chup means complete perfection or consummation. It means that since all mental afflictions are gone for good, there is a complete flowering of all virtuous qualities. There are different ways in which the term *jangchup* is used. Principally, it refers to the awakening of a bodhisattva, which can refer to any of the *bhumis* (the levels or stages a bodhisattva goes through to reach enlightenment). That is known as temporary awakening. Then there is what is called ultimate awakening, which is buddhahood.

STUDENT: Is there a point of no return, a point of ignorance from which there is no escape? Since, as I believe, we are the sole creator of our own suffering, doesn't it necessitate some kind of intervention from outside, even though it might seem that we can only get ourselves out?

RINPOCHE: There is not any kind of irreversible ignorance, because ignorance itself is not a stable, permanent, unchanging thing. It is simply a condition of your mind, an absence of recognition rather than a thing or substance. Therefore, really there is no such thing as irreversible ignorance. On the other hand, there certainly appears to be! This is because ignorance is continuous; it does not stop and start. As long as we have not reversed it, it is irreversible and it will not just disappear.

However, if we undertake what is necessary to remove it, then it is reversible or removable because ignorance is really just a process. It is an event or a continuous series of events that occur in reliance upon a variety of objects and situations. In other words, it is interdependent. It is not really a thing; it is rather like different things mixed together that produce our particular way of experiencing whatever we are undergoing. Therefore, although ignorance never started and will not cease by itself, its nature has arising and cessation, which happen all the time. The process itself will never cease until we reverse it. But we must remember that although the process is persistent and continuous, it is impermanent.

The remedy we use to counteract ignorance and produce awakening is also interdependent and based on the application of conditions. In other words, since ignorance is simply a reaction to conditions, you start by changing the conditions. This is where the influence of others comes in. You can get yourself out, but you need help.

STUDENT: Sometimes I recognize mental afflictions beforehand and can avoid them. Sometimes I recognize them when I am in the midst of them, and it's like a thunderstorm—there isn't much I can do about it. My question is twofold: First, are there different remedies for different mental afflictions? And second, when I am in the midst of my kleshas and it is intense like a thunderstorm, is it appropriate to simply be peaceful about it and think, "Well, it will be over soon?"

RINPOCHE: If you recognize that the nature of mental afflictions is unestablished, that they have no inherent existence, then you do not need any strategy or particular applications for specific instances.

However, in terms of different remedies for specific afflictions, generally speaking, if you are suffering from bewilderment, the antidote is to generate more insight. In the case of dealing with attachment, there are different approaches. For beginners, what is principally recommended is trying to alleviate the perversion of perception which leads to that kind of fixation. In other words, you should stop seeing that which is impure as pure, and stop perverting the way you experience the world. With regard to aversion and aggression, you start by thinking about what happens when you get angry and the problems that result. From a mahayana point of view, you transform aversion into patience. It is recommended that you use aversion as fuel for the development of patience as well as the strength and courage that go along with patience. But if you get rid of ignorance there will be no problem, just as you can pile up all the wood you want, but if there is no fire the wood is never going to burn.

As to what to do when you are in the midst of an overwhelmingly powerful mental affliction, the mahayana approach is to use your intelligence, your capacity for analysis and recognition. For example, if you become extremely angry, you could look directly at the anger. Looking at it, you might try to see if it exists. If it does exist, it should *be* somewhere, either inside or outside yourself. If it is one of those two places, exactly where is it? If it is somewhere, which of course it has to be, it must have a shape and it must occupy a certain amount of space. How big is your anger? What color is your anger? When you keep looking in this way, you cannot find it anywhere, and in the short run the anger may have calmed down a bit while you were looking for it. As you become trained in this kind of analysis, you gradually stumble upon the fact that the kleshas do not really exist.

If you are getting angry at another person, then the mahayana approach is to think that anyone who is your enemy is really a friend. This is because the mahayana point of view is that the development, generation, and strengthening of bodhicitta[4] depends primarily upon the development of patience. Therefore, the only possible situation in which you can really develop the kind of patience that mahayana practitioners need is one in which someone is being aggressive towards you. Therefore, whoever is aggressive with you is providing you with the conditions you need in order to practice, and I mean *really* practice. As a result, whoever appears to be your enemy is in fact the basis for your accumulation of merit, and is helping you tremendously. Now, why should you repay someone else's help with harm?

Another way mahayana practitioners look at this is to say that it is your own fault for thinking you exist! This is the kind of analysis used. It sounds odd when I explain it, and you cannot exactly use it on the spot when you get angry, but if you train yourself continually in this way of thinking, you can break down and break through the misconceptions that lead to mental afflictions.

STUDENT: Can you say something about how meditation practice cultivates compassion and insight?

RINPOCHE: The cultivation of tranquility is definitely necessary in order to generate true insight and compassion. However, whether

---

4   Literally, the mind of enlightenment. Bodhicitta is discussed in detail in the chapter on the bodhisattva path.

or not tranquility itself will generate these qualities depends upon the motivation of the practitioner. If by cultivating tranquility all you want is to become more and more tranquil, then you are not going to accomplish any insight or compassion. All you will accomplish is more tranquility. In fact, most of the meditation practices that are currently taught consist of just this cultivation of absorption in static tranquility.

On the other hand, you may apply this tranquility one-pointedly on whatever object it is placed in order to develop insight and compassion. If you apply tranquility by combining it with intelligent analysis and development of compassion, then tranquility will naturally lead to stable insight and stable compassion.

Tranquility meditation is a little bit like a knife: if you sharpen a knife, you can cut anything with it. But if you do not cut anything with it, if you keep on sharpening it forever, then sharpening the knife will not actually cut anything. However, if you make use of the knife, it will be very sharp and efficient. In the same way, shamata is the necessary companion to all virtue and goodness because a stable shamata enables you to practice anything. It enables you to generate the result of the practice and to actually make things work.

Student: Could you say more about how one develops compassion in your tradition?

Rinpoche: It starts with recognizing our own suffering. We have to begin by honestly seeing what we are going through. When we understand our suffering and where it comes from, then when we look at others we see they are basically going through the same experience. If we really see that other people are going through the same suffering as we are, we will naturally generate compassion. So compassion comes from the recognition that everyone is basically the same as we are, that we are not different from anyone else.

STUDENT: Would you say more about what you mean when you say that the self does not exist? Also, if the self does not exist, what does?

RINPOCHE: Well, there are bodies and there are minds. You know you have a body and you have a mind. We can say that these exist in some sense. As for the self, it either has to be one of those, both of those, or neither of those. The way to arrive at an understanding of what it means to say that self does not exist is to examine whether or not any of those things are really possible.

This is not something you are going to figure out instantly. It takes analysis. What you have to do is actually look: If there is a self, where is it? What is it? What does it look like? Does it have any substantial existence? If it does, it must be perceptible, and if it does not, what does that mean? You have to analyze this whole imputed self to determine its characteristics and whether something with those characteristics could actually exist. Then eventually, through that analysis, you come to some experience of what all those words mean.

STUDENT: Could you say something about interdependence?

RINPOCHE: Interdependence just means relativity. It refers to the fact that things have their particular qualities in relation to the qualities of other things. For example, if I want to snap my fingers, I use my thumb and middle finger. When the snap happens, the sound is not coming from either the thumb or the middle finger. Nevertheless, there is a sound. The sound did not come from one specific part. It came from the relation of the parts.

Compassion and Loving-Kindness as Remedies for Anger and Jealousy

THE ETHICAL FOUNDATIONS OF PRACTICE

Since anger and jealousy are perhaps the most painful mental afflictions, I would like to say a bit more about them, and specifically how to use compassion and loving-kindness as remedies.

Buddhism speaks about how to remove neuroses, which are also known as the three poisons. Loving-kindness and compassion are the most effective remedies for the three poisons, because they are the polar opposite of them. If we maintain an attitude of compassion for all living beings, there is literally no room to develop anger and hatred. Of course, the compassion we generate must not be artificial, but should come from the depths of our hearts. And by developing pure, sincere loving-kindness, we have no room to develop jealousy or other kleshas. Developing loving-kindness, we wish other beings success, and when another being is successful, we are not jealous of that success.

Applying a remedy in this way simply means to turn your mind in a different direction. Having understood the importance of developing loving-kindness and compassion as remedies, we should practice training ourselves in them over and over until we become familiar with this method. Without being completely trained in this method, there may be a lack of sincerity or confidence in that outlook. However, through diligence and consistent practice, we can develop genuine, sincere loving-kindness and compassion.

Sometimes we may doubt that we will ever be able to develop true loving-kindness and compassion. Or we may see a very cruel person, someone who we have never seen smile in many years, and say, "That person has no heart, no loving-kindness or compassion at all. It is impossible for such a person to really develop love and care for any living being." Neither is true. First of all, from the animal to the human realm, we know that everyone loves their children. Both animals and humans take care of their children, so all beings show love. Even if they do not love other people, they love their children. Second, and most important, everybody loves themselves. So love is there. It is just a question of turning self-love upside down, turning it into other-love. It is that simple. It is not true that some people have no love at all; they just never try to open their minds to the love that is there.

Shantideva taught that if we do not understand the key point in terms of attitude, then suffering cannot cease. The main point, and the most important attitude, is to open your heart, to extend loving-kindness and compassion to all living beings rather than turning it inwards and just loving yourself. The mistake that a lot of people make is that they only love themselves. They may wish to obtain peace and happiness this way, but they do not understand that all living beings are equally looking for such happiness. Not knowing this, such people complain about others, and sometimes they lock themselves away from others, thinking that all the pain and suffering surrounding them is caused by other living beings. However, no matter how much they try to run away, the world is full of living beings, and they will always end up in some sort of relationship with them. Then they spend their time complaining about this person or that person, and so forth. There is no end to it.

Instead, if we could open ourselves, trying to be helpful and caring and giving more consideration to others than to ourselves, then gradually all other beings will begin to love and care for us as well as for themselves. Because we have been extremely kind and gentle, people do not develop negative attitudes about us. Other beings start to like us, not only human beings, but also birds and animals. It is a fact that kind, gentle people are often surrounded by birds and animals that come toward them without fear. If a negative person approaches animals, no matter how much such a person beckons, they run away. The result of opening yourself and giving more consideration to others is that you really can remove your difficulties and pain.

Giving consideration to others is the mahayana attitude. This attitude was strongly practiced in the Tibetan culture. Tibetans practiced loving-kindness and compassion without distinguishing between friends and enemies, extending it equally to all living beings. They did this with the knowledge that each of us has one thing in common, the desire to obtain happiness.

Taking the attitude of loving-kindness and compassion to all beings equally, even to our enemies, as well as our relatives and friends, is part of the essential practice of bodhicitta, which we will discuss in more detail throughout this book. By training ourselves over and over in developing such an attitude, we familiarize ourselves with it. When we are able to develop this attitude and understand how precious it is, then no matter what emotion we experience, whether we are happy, sad, frustrated, angry, or anything else, we can still hold onto the attitude of giving loving-kindness and compassion. This is what it means to persevere in bodhicitta.

If we can hold onto the attitude of wishing to help others regardless of our emotional state, that is what it means to be on the bodhisattva path. A bodhisattva is a being who always has love and compassion for all living beings. Often, when people are feeling powerful or prosperous, they are willing to help others, but when they become unsuccessful and experience failure, they develop anger and frustration toward others and they forget about this precious attitude. This should not happen to a bodhisattva; their commitment is to always wish to benefit all living beings. To keep that commitment regardless of your emotional state is what it means to be a genuine bodhisattva.

Of course, being at the beginning level of our practice, we cannot fulfill desires or grant blessings as advanced bodhisattvas can. However, if we maintain our commitment of extending loving-kindness and compassion to all beings, wishing to give others happiness, and keeping this intention purely from the bottom of our hearts at all times regardless of our emotional state, this eventually leads us to become true bodhisattvas.

Our negative actions of body, speech, and mind have caused harm to beings. Conversely, our skillful and compassionate actions of body, speech, and mind will cause living beings to develop and turn towards the path of liberation. Knowing that negative actions lead us to experience more suffering, we should turn away from such activity and turn towards virtuous actions that lead us toward the path of complete liberation. Then, even if our virtuous actions are tiny and limited, we will still be accumulating positive karma day by day. Even if we only meditate 10 to 15 minutes per day, if we have a pure attitude, we will accumulate and store positive karma, which will eventually lead us to ripen the complete mind of buddhahood.

We may think that we want to progress quickly, but if our minds are not pure, we will not progress much at all, even if we practice intensely. In this situation, our practice would be like a vessel with holes in the bottom: even if we quickly pour a lot of water into the vessel, we will not fill it. On the other hand, if we have a clean vessel, perfectly made with no holes, even if we only put in one sesame seed a day, the vessel will one day be filled with seeds. The contents will be pure and clean because the vessel was perfect. Therefore, if we know the method, we can be confident that we will develop ourselves completely through the gradual process of daily practice, even if we do not practice for long periods of time. This is how we begin on the path, by understanding and learning how to enter into the gate of Dharma.

If we develop the pure, authentic mahayana attitude, it is quite definite that our accumulation will increase, and eventually be quite great. Otherwise, even if we have entered the gate of Dharma, if we take refuge simply for ourselves, we cannot say whether such practice will be helpful or not. To practice with such an attitude would be like leaving gold or diamonds unprotected in a crowd. If we leave them and come back later, some thief will most likely have taken them.

In this analogy, the gem is our merit and the thief is our anger. If we practice and accumulate merit, we might not dedicate that merit for the benefit of others but just work for ourselves. But then, the moment we develop anger toward anyone, all the merit we have accumulated is wiped away, destroyed completely. The precious gem is gone. Also, practicing with the desire to benefit only ourselves cannot be beneficial in the future. Therefore we should direct our practice to the benefit of all living beings. Especially at the end of our practice sessions, we should make the dedication, "May whatever merit I have accumulated be beneficial to all beings as vast as the skies. May they all obtain equal merit from my practice." If we do this, our merit will become inexhaustible.

Many teachers and spiritual friends in Tibet advise their students that the method of practice is more important than which particular practice we do. If we know the importance of an altruistic attitude, then whatever practice we do will be on the right path. If we do not know the importance of the correct attitude, even if we are doing an advanced practice, we will not really be following the mahayana way. The mahayana way of practice is to know that we must never forget the countless numbers of sentient beings at the beginning, the middle, and the end of practice. We should always have an altruistic attitude towards them, wishing benefit for them throughout whatever practice we are doing.

By remembering these points and working with these skillful means, we can relate to the mahayana path as a gradual process. Even good land will only produce crops if we plant the seeds and work diligently. Just having fertile land alone is not sufficient because the land will not produce crops by itself. And even if we had a wonderful harvest this year, we will again need to work hard to get the same or better harvest the following year.

Having such a motivation is the basis for the mahayana teachings. We need to put effort into actual practice to bring about results. By making this kind of effort, we become strong like a lion cub. When a cub grows up it becomes an adult lion – very powerful and strong. The analogy of the cub and lion is used frequently in the Buddha's teachings, and the teachings of the Buddha are often referred to as "The Lion's Roar." We can use this analogy to inspire us and help us to practice diligently.

QUESTIONS AND ANSWERS

STUDENT: I would like to ask about the relationship between compassion, loving-kindness, and wisdom. Isn't it possible that one could have a very pure motive, wanting to help with a very open heart, yet not have wisdom and understanding? In that case, could we do harm rather than good, even though our motive is pure? How can we bring these two together and integrate them?

RINPOCHE: That is a very good question. The situation you describe happens many times. However, if you develop loving-kindness for all living beings as limitless as the sky, not discriminating between good or bad, near or far, then wisdom will also be present in your actions. Applying this method, you cannot stray onto any wrong path. If on the other hand you have only developed loving-kindness and compassion for certain individuals, then you have to be extremely careful. In that case, you really need to bring in more wisdom.

STUDENT: It seems that we can only take compassion and love as far as our own clarity. We cannot be really compassionate in the deepest sense of the word if we have not cleaned ourselves of our own neurotic habits. So I imagine the two, wisdom and compassion, would grow together. Is this true?

RINPOCHE: If I understand correctly, what you say is quite correct. However, I may not have understood what you were trying to say, so let me try to make it clearer. If you are aware that developing loving-kindness and compassion for others is a positive thing to do, that awareness itself is clarity. Because they are interdependent, developing such an attitude is good.

STUDENT: You talked about practicing and training the mind, using loving-kindness as an antidote for jealousy, and compassion as an antidote for anger. Is it really so simple? For instance, if I was walking down the street and feeling jealous, could I stop that thought in my mind and begin to feel loving-kindness?

RINPOCHE: If we have trained ourselves to develop compassion for all living beings equally, then because of the strength of that training, whatever might cause us to develop anger instead leads us to develop compassion. If we meet someone in the street who might be a cause for developing anger, we develop compassion instead. We understand that all living beings are suffering and their minds are deluded, so we develop compassion for them, and we wish to remove their suffering.

In your case, if you meet someone on the street who is very annoying verbally or physically, you can understand how deluded and confused that person is. Understanding this, you could feel sympathy and compassion instead of getting angry. That is how one is the remedy for the other. The more you learn about the neuroses of sentient beings, the more compassion you will develop. You understand that their minds are deluded, and you see that they create negative actions out of their confusion.

Generally, mothers love their children, right? When a child has mental problems, she loves the child even more. Even if the child does strange things, she realizes that those actions are caused by the child's problems, and she tries to find other methods to help that child. Similarly, if you know about the deluded minds of sentient beings, beings who do not know how to turn themselves to a positive path, there is no room for anger or hatred once you have trained yourself in the meditative state of loving-kindness and compassion.

STUDENT: You are presenting this from the point of view of someone who has already overcome anger, but when someone like me who is untrained walks along the street, I *do* feel angry. Should I then think something different?

RINPOCHE: First of all, I would like to make it clear that we are speaking about meditation, and therefore we need to train in everything. We cannot change ourselves overnight, not having any anger, hatred, or jealousy at all. It takes time to overcome such things. Second, we have to prepare ourselves for these occasions. When we are alone and are not feeling anger, hatred, or jealousy, we have to reflect on these emotions and their results. We come to understand that if we explode with anger, hatred, or jealousy, the result is never peaceful. The result is always something harmful both for ourselves and other beings, and does not really give peace or happiness to either. Therefore, as Dharma practitioners we have to understand the importance of controlling our negative actions, and the way to do this is to always be mindful of the negative results of negative actions. Here we are primarily discussing anger, but the same can be said for any of the other poisons as well.

If we are mindful, then if something happens as we are walking down the street, we do not react by exploding. Being mindful and aware, we know how to control ourselves. If we have not been mindful in the past, if we have not prepared ourselves by contemplating, then it is hard to control anger when it arises. This is just like if we have a hole in our roof and neglect to fix it before it rains. When the rain does start, it is too hard to go out and fix the roof. Therefore, it is best to prepare before things happen. Keeping this mindfulness all the time is really the best practice for the beginner. As well, we also have to train in compassion as much as possible, trying our best to develop compassion for all living beings.

STUDENT: You said that we know everyone loves because everyone loves their children. I have also read that all mothers love their children in Buddhist books. This bothers me because I see children who are not loved by their mothers, children who are battered, abused, and starved. And I see children who don't seem to love their parents, who perhaps have been abused by their parents. It is not the norm, but it happens.

RINPOCHE: That is real evidence of the result of and power of anger. We have to understand that our hatred and anger are very damaging. This is the main reason we say that anger and jealousy are the root of all our troubles, and it is also why we emphasize learning how to control such neuroses through meditation. When we are unable to control these feelings, when we explode with anger, we may hurt the people we love, and sometimes we even hurt ourselves. Especially in the earlier stages of our practice, we have to be very cautious, and remain mindful of how important it is to control our anger.

Generally, all the suffering of war is caused by anger and jealousy. We know that each nation tries to build schools and medical centers to develop their own country and make their people happy; they try to care for the sick and the elderly, and so forth. Then suddenly because of jealousy and anger, two nations go to war. In the war, one nation destroys everything that it took the other a hundred years to build. That is an example of why it can be said that anger and jealousy are the roots of all difficulties on earth.

STUDENT: Is there a difference between love and compassion?

RINPOCHE: The Buddhist tradition draws a distinction between these two concepts in the following way: Love or loving-kindness is the notion of wanting to give happiness to other beings. It is loving-kindness to want to give any happiness, such as kind words, material possessions, and so forth. Because of loving-kindness, we rejoice at whatever wealth or property others may have, and because of this rejoicing, feelings of jealousy are eliminated.

Compassion is wanting someone to be liberated from pain, suffering, and frustration. We want to liberate every being from whatever suffering they are experiencing—physical, mental, and so forth. Therefore, compassion is the remedy for anger, because in anger we develop the wish to harm others, whereas with compassion we wish to liberate others from pain.

STUDENT: Could you say a little bit more about how shamata relates to bodhicitta and how bodhicitta practice relates to the development of vipasyana?

RINPOCHE: As was said by Lord Tsongkhapa, the great Buddhist master who founded the Gelugpa Lineage:

Shamata is a state of mind in which when the mind is at rest, it is immovable like the king of mountains. When sent out, it alights upon whatever virtuous object one chooses and enters into it with one's full control.

Of course, from a mahayana point of view, the main object of virtue is the generation of bodhicitta. Thus, in order to generate bodhicitta and increase it, shamata is beneficial and definitely necessary. It is what enables us to actually go through the process of generating bodhicitta.

As far as the connection between the development of bodhicitta and vipasyana, practically speaking, when you practice bodhicitta you are really practicing compassion, and compassion and insight are closely related. You cannot have total insight without being softened up by compassion and you cannot have full compassion without insight. This is because the commitment of bodhicitta, that heroic commitment through which someone is willing to take on the suffering of all beings and is willing to do anything to liberate all sentient beings, has to depend upon the removal of ego-clinging, the removal of the false imputation of his or her own inherent existence. As long as we are stuck in materialism, as long as we are stuck in ego-clinging, we cannot possibly make that commitment because it would be too terrifying. Of course, the only way someone can transcend ego-clinging and materialism is through insight. Bodhicitta really does depend upon vipasyana, and vipasyana also depends upon bodhicitta. They work together.

The Importance of Mind Training Practice

People who are not familiar with Buddhism are sometimes dismayed when they hear about the ten virtuous and unvirtuous actions of body, speech, and mind. They may think, "How can I possibly do that? It's impossible to change from these ten unvirtuous actions to the ten virtuous actions." This is where we need to apply the shamata practice of sitting meditation. We have seen that it is possible to progress toward a virtuous life by developing the mindfulness that comes out of shamata, which basically involves developing concentration. However, after developing the stability of sitting meditation, it is necessary to train your mind. In Tibetan, mind training is known as *lojong*.

First, we train the mind by awakening its loving-kindness and compassion, and we do this by contemplating what we most desire. Naturally, we think of happiness, good health, and freedom from fear and insecurity. We then try to extend this contemplation to what our families want. We see that they want the same things: they would also like to have good health, success, and happiness. From there, we consider what any human being wants, and we see that all human beings want these things as well. Expanding our thinking process further, we consider the wishes of animals, including reptiles, birds, fish, and so forth. Although we typically draw a line between humans and non-humans, we see that all beings want the same thing that we want, which is happiness.

Then, still sitting, we feel sympathy for every living being as we realize, "All of them want exactly what I do." As a result of this feeling, our envious thoughts disappear, and we feel more like sharing. We also realize that all along we have been sharing something we were not even aware of: our desire for happiness. When we see this, there is no ill-will or harmful thoughts towards others, because the moment we consider that everyone wants the same things as we do, we will not want to harm them. With this understanding, the natural energy of love and compassion grows.

The three mental afflictions of attachment, anger, and ignorance are very powerful, and they have led us to engage in the negative actions of body, speech, and mind. Therefore, we need to find a remedy for these three patterns so we can avoid them. But we do not need to find specific methods to apply to each particular emotion as long as we are able to awaken the energy of loving-kindness and compassion. When we consider that all beings including ourselves desire happiness, we develop a sympathetic feeling towards all beings and love for others begins to grow. This energy is the very remedy for attachment and hatred.

Second, we can extend the contemplation of what we most desire to consider what we would most like to avoid. We would like to avoid any harm, misfortune, or poor health. In the same way as before, we gradually extend that feeling to all beings, who also wish to avoid harm, misfortune, and poor health. We consider that animals, birds, and so forth also feel this way. This naturally leads us to wish that all beings, including ourselves, could avoid harm. This pacifies hatred because we know that hatred leads us to harm others, and we now understand that others do not wish to be harmed. Further, we understand that harming others harms ourselves. In the long term we can fully uproot attachment and hatred, but at the beginning we simply start by weakening their power.

Third, we apply a remedy for ignorance. There are several ways to do this. Having the knowledge of what constitutes virtuous and unvirtuous actions eliminates ignorance, as does the knowledge of what is positive and what is negative. Ignorance is also eliminated by knowing that your pain, misfortune, and suffering in this life are due to having engaged in negative actions of body, speech, and mind in the past. As well, it also eliminates ignorance to know that if you enjoy well-being, goodness, and freedom from sickness in the present, this is due to having engaged in positive actions in a past life. Similarly, it eliminates ignorance to know that if we engage in positive actions in this life, we will enjoy positive things and be free from suffering in the next life. It also eliminates ignorance to know that if we engage in negative actions in this life, this will cause us to experience suffering in the next life. The knowledge of how the past relates to the present and the present to the future is the elimination of ignorance.

Having learned that what we desire is the same thing that all other living beings desire, and that what we want to avoid is the same thing that all other living beings want to avoid, our love and compassion for all living beings is energized. Based upon this, we pray that all sentient beings obtain the causes of happiness, and this prayer energizes our loving-kindness. We also pray for all sentient beings to be liberated from the causes of suffering, which further energizes our compassion. This is how we develop love and compassion, and this also eliminates ignorance.

At a more advanced level of meditation practice, the elimination of ignorance is also connected with the recognition of shunyata, the empty nature of all phenomena. We will not go into this in detail here, but I want you to know that ignorance is also eliminated by recognizing the fact that phenomena have no concrete, substantial identity. However, at this beginning level, the elimination of ignorance refers to knowing what is positive and what is negative, and learning to have proper love and compassion for living beings.

Our teacher, Shakyamuni Buddha, presents us with an orderly set of stages of practice. He emphasizes that students should progress along the path in a smooth manner, and not skip any stages. He explained that these three stages are: first, to learn to practice positive actions; second, to learn to subdue attachment to the personal self; and third, to attempt to recognize the empty nature of all phenomena.

At present, we have not really fully developed ourselves in practicing the positive actions of body, speech, and mind. At this stage if you want to learn about emptiness, it could be like jumping off the top of a mountain because you think you can fly. However, you have no wings, and you know what the result of that would be! In order to fly, you have to develop wings. The proper manner to develop wings in this example is first to accumulate the benefits of doing positive actions, then to remove fixation on the ego, and finally, gain insight into the empty nature of all phenomena.

THE PRACTICE OF TONGLEN

The purpose of the statement "Pacify your mind" is to make it possible to avoid unvirtuous actions and perform virtuous actions. Completely pacifying your mind means to develop the calm abiding nature of mind. Having pacified the mind, we should not fall back to the neurotic style of mind that we had before we trained ourselves. When this training becomes solid and strong due to consistent practice, we have pacified our minds completely.

In the context of the bodhisattva path, we speak of resting the mind in the samadhi of love and compassion. The real meaning of resting the mind in this samadhi is similar to the contemplation in which we realize that all living beings desire happiness and freedom from suffering just as we do. Feeling equally the desires of every living being, we rest in that state with a sense of love and compassion.

The purpose of resting in such a state is to understand and become more open towards the needs of others, rather than just being aware of our own needs. Not only do we become open in this way, but we also realize that all other beings need these things to the same degree that we do. From this we effortlessly develop a feeling of accepting every being and every situation with love and compassion, without harshness. Because we have developed this acceptance, if we further train in tonglen, where we exchange ourselves with others, the result can be quite powerful and magnificent.

Training is always necessary. If you experience meditative stability and feel acceptance for every being but do not train in exchanging yourself for others, there will not be any strength to that feeling. Exchanging yourself does not necessarily mean that you totally exchange your body with the body of someone else. You do not totally transform yourself from the inside out, so to speak; nothing is really being exchanged. Rather, we accept that every living being needs the same things that we do, and therefore we accept their needs and are not blind to them. As a result, we are also open to giving whatever they need.

At the beginning, however, training is very important in order to get accustomed to the idea of openness. Unless we train our minds well, our acceptance, exchanging, and willingness to give may not be genuine. The tonglen practice, which is also known as sending and receiving, will make our approach pure.

The technique for doing tonglen is as follows: As you exhale, imagine that all the virtue, merit, goodness, success, pleasure, and every favorable condition you have is shared with every living being. As you inhale, breathe in every hardship, frustration, disease, and all of the unfavorable conditions that exist in the entire universe. When you do this, you train your mind to accept negative things and let go of positive things.

We do this mind training in order to prepare for actual situations when we will have the opportunity to give and receive. When we see someone suffering, we always feel sympathy. We would like to help, but because we are not free from mental afflictions, after we offer help we sometimes regret what we have done. We may feel that we should not have given what we gave, or that we gave too much. That kind of regret is often a sign of not being fully prepared. The tonglen practice is essential in order to be well-prepared.

The manner in which someone practices tonglen is also based upon their strength of mind. Someone who has a warrior-like mind is willing to send merit, virtue, goodness, and success to all living beings, particularly to his or her greatest enemy. Sharing such merit with someone whom you regard as your worst enemy shows great strength of mind. For others who do not have such strength of mind, the idea of sharing good things with their enemy is very difficult to accept, let alone actually do. Individuals have different mental capacities, which are based partly upon how strongly they train their minds.

Some people think this practice is merely a mental game. I have heard students complain about this, saying, "What is the benefit of just mentally giving everything positive to the world and taking in everything negative?" The point of tonglen is that we develop a habit and familiarize our minds with this approach. Tonglen turns us into very strong individuals: it helps us to let go of positive things and to accept negative things. Although it seems to be merely mental training, it is not only that, for the more consistently we train our minds, the more we are able to cope with good and bad situations in our daily lives. As a result of tonglen, when we actually give or receive, we do not close down, and there is no hesitation. If we become strong and effective individuals in our work and in society, every action we take will naturally be quite meaningful.

TONGLEN AS A REMEDY FOR
THE MENTAL AFFLICTIONS, FEAR, AND INSECURITY

Becoming well-trained in the tonglen practice is a potent remedy for pacifying mental afflictions. For example, we have strong attachments because we cling to things that are appealing. Naturally we should appreciate good things, but there is a difference between appreciation and clinging; clinging is not just enjoyment, it is more like possessiveness. By training ourselves in tonglen, we do not try to possess things but learn to let them go. Attachment is naturally pacified when we do this as opposed to clinging to things. If we see something beautiful, we appreciate it but do not cling to it. Tonglen gives us this capacity.

You may also wonder why people are so arrogant. We tend to think that we are the only person in the universe, thinking, "I am the best, most charismatic individual in the whole world." When we practice tonglen, however, we become more accepting. We learn about the needs and qualities of others, therefore pacifying the attitude of arrogance.

With respect to anger and hatred, anger is generally a momentary experience which can nevertheless cause great harm. When anger is entrenched it turns to hatred, and in this form it can be extremely destructive. Often we experience anger or hatred from a protective mind, becoming angry because we think that someone threatens or has already taken our pleasure, goodness, or something else that we possess. We might act out our anger as a way to prevent these people from taking more. However, when we have practiced tonglen effectively and have learned to let go, we have nothing to protect. Not only have we let go, but we have accepted all manner of misfortune, illness, and unfavorable condition into ourselves. We no longer need to protect ourselves and our possessions and, as a result, we pacify the cause of these types of anger and hatred.

As for thoughts of ill-will connected with jealousy, these typically come from the inability to rejoice at the success and well-being that others possess. We actually feel bad when someone experiences good fortune. However, if we are willing to give away everything positive that we possess, this should eliminate jealous feelings when someone else has good fortune. This is how tonglen pacifies the emotion of jealousy.

Finally, we might wonder how tonglen addresses ignorance. Basically, once we are well-trained, our minds are open: we are no longer arrogant or selfish, and we no longer only think of our own needs instead of those of others. Understanding and caring about the needs of others, accepting them and being willing to share with them, and seeing the equality of all living beings is wisdom. This cuts through ignorance.

In addition to these mental afflictions, it is very common to suffer from insecurity and various fears or phobias. What is the cause of all this insecurity and fear? We are constantly afraid to make mistakes, constantly afraid that we might have to face criticism.

This creates a tremendous pressure that is hard to avoid and hard to live with. Tonglen can helps overcome this kind of problem, because once we are willing to accept the misfortune, illness, and mistakes of the whole universe, we will not be bothered by our own shortcomings and mistakes. Therefore, tonglen also eliminates fear and feelings of insecurity.

The great master Shantideva[5] mentioned that tonglen practice is also very affordable! Because it is a mental practice in which we give everything away mentally, it does not compromise our financial well-being. We simply let go with our minds. If we practice tonglen properly, the effect is more beneficial than offering material gifts, because we learn to overcome the mental afflictions. This is why Shantideva taught that if we do this mind training accurately, even though it may seem like imaginary play, it will have a tremendous effect on our mental strength and help us overcome the mental afflictions.

TONGLEN AS A REMEDY FOR NEGATIVE ACTIONS

Without knowing the key points of mind training or, more generally, if we engage in any Dharma practice without understanding its point, we might end up mistaking the practice of non-virtue for the practice of virtue. Therefore, Shantideva also emphasized that we need to be very cautious. We should examine our minds: Are the things we think and the things we do truly sincere and positive? If not, we need to look at that. This is the key to all remedies.

It may seem quite difficult to avoid the ten negative actions, but for a sincere tonglen practitioner it becomes quite simple. In tonglen practice, we train our minds to love and therefore benefit all sentient beings by sharing our positive qualities. By doing so, we naturally lessen our desire to engage in the ten negative actions.

For example, the first negative action of body is killing. If we love living beings and want to benefit them, the idea of killing is simply not there. Therefore, it is natural to abandon killing.

5   A great Indian bodhisattva who is best known for his writings on the conduct of a bodhisattva.

The second negative action of body is stealing. Since we have developed the wish to give generously based upon the realization that others have needs and suffer just as we do, the desire to take something that belongs to someone else does not arise.

The third is sexual misconduct. Engaging in sexual misconduct brings tremendous pain to your partner and others. Since the point of the tonglen training is the wish to benefit others and avoid hurting them, the effect of the training would be to reduce the actual inclination to engage in sexual misconduct.

Therefore, once we have trained our minds properly with tonglen practice, we can avoid the negative actions of body effortlessly. Mind training is essential for working with all aspects of our behavior. It tames the mental afflictions such that they no longer have control over us. If mental afflictions have control over us, we have no choice but to engage in killing, stealing, sexual misconduct, and so forth. But if we have control over the mental afflictions, our actions become a matter of choice. This is the main reason that training the mind is important, because this training allows us to have control over mental afflictions. Eventually, we can uproot them completely.

TONGLEN AS THE GROUND FOR DEVELOPING BODHICITTA AND PRAJNA

Mahayana practice is designed to help us develop the completely awakened state of mind. Through such practice, we develop ourselves so that we can benefit all living beings. The bodhisattvas and enlightened beings of the past started their practice in the same way that we are starting to practice: doing tonglen, learning to understand the equality of all living beings, avoiding negative actions of body, speech, and mind, and making a commitment to practice the corresponding positive actions. By practicing in this way, they were able to awaken the enlightened energy of mind and benefit limitless beings. However, if our goal is not a positive one, then even if we apply the highest tantric practices, they will not lead us to experience enlightenment. Whether we actually benefit or harm others is due to our intentions.

There is a story which shows the result of applying deity practices with the aim of harming others. Long ago in Tibet, there was an ugly little man who was picked on by the people in his village. He was very angry at these people, so he took up a deity practice with the intention of gaining enough power to destroy them in his next life. As a result of these negative aspirations, he took rebirth in the eastern part of Tibet. He became a powerful king who ruled his subjects in a very cruel manner, torturing and destroying thousands. This was the outcome of his misdirected practice, based upon his negative intentions while performing it.

Therefore, if the motivation behind your practice is not positive, even the highest practices may not lead you to a good result. Many practices, particularly the higher practices, are very powerful, like a gun. If you keep a gun in your home for protection, it does not necessarily harm anyone. However, if you fire it, it could certainly harm someone, and whether anyone is harmed depends upon where you aim. Just as you could harm yourself and others with a gun, the higher vajrayana practices can be dangerous. If we do not do them with the proper aim, then even if we think we are protecting ourselves, we might end up destroying ourselves instead.

Having the proper attitude of mind is very simple: just train the mind in accordance with the tonglen practice. This tonglen approach is the application of bodhicitta or enlightened mind, always being willing to share things with others and never excluding anyone. As long as we do not have a selfish attitude, we will not make any mistakes in this practice. That is the key to the higher practices: we must maintain enlightened mind, the supreme compassionate mind. Tonglen is crucial to developing this. You may think that tonglen is a simple practice, but it is required on every level of the path, in the hinayana, mahayana, and vajrayana, so do not underestimate it.

As we advance in tonglen practice, pure knowledge or prajna takes birth within us. Before we were fixated on ego and duality, believing that everything was real, solid, and concrete. As long as we feel that everything, including our self-identity, is real, suffering and problems spring up. Usually our senses and the objects that we perceive come into contact momentarily, and after this initial meeting we experience attraction or aversion to the object. However, if there is pure knowledge, there will not be any fixation either upon the solid existence of the object or the experience of the sense perception that perceives it.

As we develop prajna, we come to understand the emptiness of all phenomena, including the personal self. Understanding the empty nature, seeing that there is no solid basis to phenomena or ourselves, we are able to fully let go, and then authentic love and compassion deepen immensely. As long as we are in a state of strong fixation, it is beyond our capacity to imagine the possible strength of our love and compassion. However the pure knowledge that transcends all such fixation can develop within us, and this pure knowledge uproots our fixation on ego.

QUESTIONS AND ANSWERS

STUDENT: My question is about practice. We discussed shamata practice as something which helps stabilize the mind. We also talked about tonglen as a way to develop compassion and reduce clinging to yourself and objects. Do you have any sort of general guideline about how we should divide our time between these two practices?

RINPOCHE: If you are a complete beginner, only shamata is necessary. In that case, the mind training in tonglen we have been discussing is not proper, because your mind is not yet ready for it. Once you have developed some shamata, some concentration, then the mind becomes calm, more receptive, and willing to let go. That is the point when you should apply tonglen. At that point shamata is important, but shamata is not the ultimate practice.

If you are somewhat experienced at shamata, you should try to alternate tonglen and shamata in accordance with your mood. Our moods are not always the same. I could say you should do them fifty-fifty, but that may not be correct in every case. When you feel calm and relaxed, try to do the tonglen practice. When your mind is excited with a lot of thoughts and you find it difficult to sit, give more time to shamata.

STUDENT: You spoke about the difference between appreciating an object and being attached to it. Are there any warning signs before we cross over the line from appreciation to attachment? Is there a way not to get so far into attachment that it is difficult to let go?

RINPOCHE: According to the teachings, it is said that the five senses are the gates of attachment. We become attached to things that look attractive, taste wonderful, sound delightful, and so on. With the five senses as the gates, there are five types of objects to which we become attached. According to the Buddhist teachings, when you see something that is very attractive, you can appreciate its goodness and beauty. What you need to do in order not to go over the line, however, is once you have appreciated the object, think that you are offering that very beauty and attractiveness to the enlightened beings. Once you have offered it, there is no notion of "I want that." When there is "I," that is where you really begin to grasp.

There is also a second approach you could take. If, for example, you see an individual with tremendous beauty, you think, "May all living beings have such beauty and attractiveness."

The point is not to block out the appreciation, but to let go of your attachment. There is nothing wrong with appreciating things.

The Refuge Vow
The Meaning of Refuge

The first step to formally enter the Buddhist path is taking refuge vows. We take refuge in the Buddha, the Dharma, and the Sangha. The term refuge is used frequently in Buddhism, and it is important to understand what this really means. It is also essential to understand the objects of refuge, including what is an authentic object of refuge and what is not.

Choosing the correct object of refuge will enable us to develop further as well as give us power, insight, and wisdom. If the object of refuge lacks power, then we cannot obtain blessings or energy from it. This is the reason we need to speak about authentic and inauthentic objects of refuge. When we take refuge in an authentic object, there are many things that we have to abandon, and many things that we can adopt and practice. The authentic object of refuge is called the object of refuge that is beyond samsara, and an inauthentic object of refuge is called the object of refuge that is within samsara.

We all know that a lion produces cubs. Because the parents of the cubs are powerful and strong, the cub grows to be as strong as its parents. However, if rabbits or mice tried to produce a lion cub, it would of course be impossible. They can only produce offspring that have the same capabilities they have, and cannot produce one who is stronger or more powerful. Similarly, if we take refuge in worldly objects, it is like hoping for rabbits or mice to give birth to a lion cub.

In the past, many people took refuge in trees, rocks, mountains, or any of the countless objects that exist in samsara. They hoped these things could remove all obstacles and grant blessings, power, and energy. However, since these objects are in samsara, and although they might have some qualities, they have no power to liberate beings from samsara. For this reason, our object of refuge should be something beyond samsara. An object beyond samsara can produce someone who is powerful like a lion, far more powerful than a rabbit. We should take refuge in higher beings that are beyond samsara, beings that can liberate us from this cyclic existence.

Although the Buddha himself mentioned that there were many beings who took refuge in lakes, trees, and mountains, until recently, I had only read about such things. However, when I visited South America, I found evidence of this teaching. When I was there, I heard that some people had taken refuge in an ocean near where they live, and there were a few people who took refuge in a mountain. One group of people even took refuge in a great general who had passed away some years before, hoping that this general could liberate them from their pain and suffering. There were also people who had taken refuge in a very skillful hunter. Seeing that, I realized how people can mistake inauthentic objects of refuge for authentic objects of refuge.

MOTIVATIONS FOR TAKING REFUGE

The successful development of each person depends upon their individual efforts. Even a lion cub cannot grow up to be as strong and powerful as its parents if the cub has some defect such as being born blind or crippled. Therefore, in order to skillfully and fruitfully develop ourselves in the spiritual path, we have to understand the three types of motivation for practicing the Dharma.

The lowest motivation for practicing the Dharma is to do so purely for selfish reasons. Someone might take refuge just for their own welfare, to be successful and powerful in this current life, and to find happiness for themselves alone. Or they might take refuge in the hope of removing their illnesses and fear without having much desire to benefit others.

This lesser motivation for taking refuge is comparable to a blind or crippled lion cub. Though born from very powerful parents, it still has this defect. If someone takes refuge for the sake of personal happiness and success in this life, they would be like that cub.

Inferior motives for taking refuge are those that are essentially self-centered. Another such motive is someone who understands that their experiences of pain, suffering, and misfortune in this life are all the result of past negative karma. Therefore, he or she hopes to have a better birth in the next life due to practice and virtuous actions. Such a person understands that he or she does not have great happiness, joy, and peace in this life for the same reason that a farm not previously cultivated will not produce crops. Seeing that there were not enough crops this year, that person works harder to get a better crop next year.

However, with this motivation of self-benefit for the next life, complete realization will not take place, even if a person takes birth in one of the higher realms such as a god realm. Even if a person understands that the pain, suffering, and misfortune they are now experiencing is the result of past negative karma, that person might still practice only for the purpose of having a better future life. This is like a cub developing his eyesight so he can see better, or developing his strength so he can walk on his own. According to the Buddhist view, this is still a very low motive for taking refuge, but it is much higher than taking refuge in a tree, rock, or mountain. We should understand, however, that our happiness in the next life is not permanent. It is like poisonous food: even if it is delicious, the result of eating such food is death. Therefore, taking this kind of refuge does not completely liberate us from suffering.

The higher form of taking refuge is taking refuge not only for ourselves, but for others. All beings have a common wish, the wish to obtain happiness and peace. We see all beings struggling to obtain such happiness. Animals do not go to work in the same way as human beings, but they are still as busy as humans trying to find happiness. Although all beings are busily trying to obtain happiness, they do not know the right way to do so, and so end up experiencing hardship and suffering.

For instance, birds fly to different places to search for food to satisfy their hunger or thirst. While they are doing so, they meet predators who attack them, and they lose their lives. In the world of animals, there is always one that preys on another, and therefore animals live in constant fear, with absolutely no feeling of security. A fish may be swimming in the ocean searching for food, and then suddenly it is caught on a hook. All it wanted was to satisfy its hunger, but instead it lost its life.

Human beings work day and night to obtain happiness, security, and overcome future problems, but we end up having more problems and difficulties. There is no end to pain and suffering through working hard on a worldly level. Those who die working to obtain happiness in this world go through tremendous hardship and feelings of loss immediately after death. They experience pain not only from the samsaric life they lived, but also pain and a feeling of loss after that life. Understanding the suffering that arises from such worldly obsession can lead us to commit to the practice of Dharma.

We know that no matter how hard people work, no matter how much they try to obtain happiness through indulging in samsaric activities, all they obtain is further pain and suffering. Seeing how blind they are, we develop loving-kindness and compassion that is not superficial, but that comes from the depth of our bones. Our loving-kindness and compassion towards them increases even more because of our knowledge that there are other methods by which they could find real happiness. We understand that they do not find the way to genuine happiness because of their blindness. Instead, they always do the opposite, which gives them pain and suffering. If we have this attitude, we have understood the main point of the mahayana way of taking refuge.

Knowing that all living beings are wandering in samsara without knowing how to permanently liberate themselves, a practitioner develops a wish to liberate them from the root of their suffering. "How happy I would be if I could liberate all the limitless sentient beings from the cause of their suffering!" With that type of motivation, we develop loving-kindness towards living beings. With that loving-kindness, we simply wish to give happiness, remove pain, and liberate all beings from the causes of pain. We develop compassion and feel the pain of sentient beings, sympathizing and understanding how difficult it is to be in samsara. We feel what it is like to be constantly in this state of frustration, pain, and dissatisfaction.

TAKING THE REFUGE VOWS

Through the power of our mental afflictions, we have been undergoing intolerable suffering in samsara since beginningless time. This is the reason we go for refuge, and it is what we seek refuge from: we seek a way to liberate ourselves from this suffering. In order to achieve this liberation, it is necessary to depend upon the protection or refuge of those who are totally without the defects of samsara, those who have entirely conquered and removed these defects. Ultimately, this refuge is the Buddha.

However, in order to obtain buddhahood, that state of liberation which is the supreme refuge, it is necessary to make use of the path that leads to it. The path consists of the Dharma, which are the teachings given by the Buddha, and these teachings lead us to freedom from the suffering of samsara and to a state of permanent peace and happiness. But we cannot enter into and practice this path simply under our own power. We need the guidance and assistance of others. That is why we also go for refuge in the Sangha or community of practitioners, those who are our companions on the path. So we go for refuge not just to the Buddha, but also to the Dharma and the Sangha.

The time reference for the vow of refuge is the thought, "I take refuge from this moment until my attainment of complete buddhahood." This is the mahayana approach. You should not go for refuge with the intention of simply obtaining your own liberation, but also to bring all sentient beings to the state of complete buddhahood.

COMMITMENTS OF REFUGE

Having taken the refuge vow, it is necessary to keep the commitments of the vow. If you take the vow and do not observe the commitments, then what would otherwise be beneficial becomes a source of problems.

The commitments are not difficult to keep. The first commitment is that having gone for refuge to the Buddha, you should treat all images of the Buddha, even those of poor quality, with respect and veneration. You should see the image as the actual Buddha, and treat it as though it were the Buddha in person.

Then, having gone for refuge to the Dharma, and particularly having done so in the mahayana manner, you should abandon harming other beings as much as you can and instead help other beings as much as you can.

Having gone for refuge in the Sangha, recognize that those who practice in the same lineage and in the same tradition are your companions not only for this life, but also from previous lives and again in future lives. You should treat other sangha members with respect, devotion, and friendliness. As well, you should avoid discriminating too much between different traditions of Dharma and even different religious traditions. You should avoid thinking, for example, "Well, we Buddhists are the smart ones, and the others are fools." Just practice what you practice and have conviction in it, but let other people practice what they practice.

GUIDELINES FOR DAILY PRACTICE

As for daily practice, you should keep an image of the Buddha in your home. At best it should be in a special room, or if not, in your bedroom. It need not be very fancy; any kind of image will do. If it is in your bedroom, your head should face in the direction of the statue, not your feet. Every day you should go in front of it and make whatever offerings you can. It is traditional to offer such things as food, water, incense, and lamps. Every morning, after making the offerings, make three prostrations toward the Buddha and then recite the refuge vow twenty-one, seven, or at least three times.

When you eat a meal, imagine that you are offering the best of the food to the Buddha, Dharma, and Sangha. If you eat with that attitude, you will attain the same merit that you would have attained if you had actually offered all that food to the Buddha in person. There is also a short meal prayer that is commonly done in which you mentally offer the food to the Three Jewels.

Whenever you begin any activity or work, think, "May this work be consecrated by the protection of the Three Jewels. May it go well and be beneficial to all beings."

When you go to sleep at night, dispose of the offerings presented that day and prepare the shrine for the offerings to be presented the next day, make three prostrations, and then go to sleep with the kind of confidence that a small child has when going to sleep in its mother's lap. Go to sleep in the state of mind that you are being embraced by the protection of the Three Jewels.

The more you can maintain an attitude of confidence in and supplication towards the Buddha, Dharma, and Sangha, the more you will experience the qualities that are associated with the act of refuge. While there is no distinction between the compassion of the Buddha, Dharma, and Sangha toward someone who prays to them and someone who does not, it is like the sun: if you keep your eyes shut, you will not see the sun; but if you open them, you will. In the same way, the more devotion and commitment you have, the more blessings you will receive.

The Four Immeasurables

ASPIRATION PRAYER OF THE FOUR IMMEASURABLES

May all sentient beings have happiness and the causes of happiness.

May all sentient beings be free from suffering
and the causes of suffering.

May all beings never be separated from the great happiness
that is free from all suffering.

May all beings experience the state of equanimity
which is free from aversion and attachment.

AN INTRODUCTION TO THE FOUR IMMEASURABLES

This prayer and practice of the Four Immeasurables is really central to Mahayana Buddhism. It is central because it expresses the profound outlook of bodhicitta. We do it to develop the vast attitude of benefiting all beings and helping them reach enlightenment.

As we have discussed, each one of us without exception has the potential to experience the awakened mind, and each one of us also has habitual obscurations. These habitual obscurations, which are self-created, are the causes of our suffering. Once we understand our potential and our shortcomings, we need to apply skillful means in order to unravel our habits of confusion and unfold our potential.

In order for this potential to bloom, we must have the right attitude and the right motivation. First, it is essential to understand that we can definitely experience enlightened mind. We have everything we need within ourselves, and we need to have firm belief in this fact. Second, we should want to share our understanding of this potential with others so that it can benefit their lives as well. Just as we possess enlightened mind, so do all beings, and our belief in this can help them realize their potential. Being motivated by a genuine interest in benefiting others is an important ground for our study of the Mahayana Dharma.

When we say, "the four immeasurables," what is really meant by "immeasurable," and what are the four? The term for immeasurable in Tibetan is *tsay may*. *Tsay* means measure, extent, or limit, and may means not or without, so together the term means immeasurable or limitless. The four things that are immeasurable are loving-kindness, compassion, sympathetic joy, and equanimity. These qualities are considered immeasurable because, in the outlook of bodhicitta, we extend them to all sentient beings, and sentient beings are limitless in number. Extending compassion, for example, to immeasurable beings, creates an immeasurable amount of compassion. That is what is meant by the Four Immeasurables.

LOVING-KINDNESS

THE first immeasurable is loving-kindness or maitri, which is *jampa* in Tibetan. We all have the quality of loving-kindness; our minds are endowed with it. But what does loving-kindness mean? According to Buddhism, it means being sensitive to the well-being of others. Each and every one of us wants to feel good. We want to have physical well-being and a healthy, sane mind. Not only do we desire this for ourselves, but for others as well. We have a genuine interest in the physical and psychological well-being of our children, parents, relatives, friends, and colleagues. Therefore, loving-kindness is the ability to have a sense of warmth and caring for the well-being of ourselves and others.

However, instead of properly developing our potential, we sometimes tend to misuse it. This is what creates all the different varieties of pain and suffering, and what obstructs our potential experience of warmth and loving-kindness. We are not talking about developing something that we do not have, because the potential for developing these experiences is already within us. But these healthy qualities of mind can become tainted by egoistic clinging. When used in this way, they become distorted and inappropriate.

We know that all sentient beings without exception yearn for physical and mental well-being. However, we are usually only interested in the well-being of a certain circle of people, and our interest has some strings attached. Our concern for their well-being comes more from our personal relationship to them, we say *my* parents, *my* children, *my* partner, *my* relatives. We say *mine* because of what they are to *me*. We have to look at this clearly, and we must acknowledge that we are not particularly interested in the well-being of other people for their own benefit. Rather, we are interested in their well-being because of who they are to us. Because of this, our concern is shaky and untrustworthy. This unstable foundation is due to the motives behind this thought, motives which do not stem from genuine, heartfelt loving-kindness. It is a type of loving-kindness, but it is twisted by the idea of *mine*.

This situation may be obvious, but we need to look at it closely, so we can introduce the necessary changes to such an attitude. When our concern for the well-being of others is based on our self-absorbed world, we draw lines and develop a fixed, grasping sense of territory. There is clinging and attachment, and where there is clinging and attachment, there is automatically aversion towards those who are "others" or outside of the "me" and "mine." Anyone outside of our territory is unwelcome, and when these others experience well-being, prosperity, or health, we feel irritated. Certainly there is something seriously wrong about the quality of such loving-kindness.

Furthermore, we may care for those in our select circle, but do we really care for them for their own sake? Usually our concern for their well-being is based on expectations of them being my "such and such." We expect they will treat us in the same way that we treat them, and thus we can be nourished by their well-being. Even this closed circle of people cannot fully trust in our loving-kindness because, although we say that we care for them, we also will develop animosity towards them when they do not maintain our image of them. When they do something questionable, our loving-kindness towards them becomes questionable as well. Rather than truly caring for their well-being, we want them to do something for us, and therefore we are not really interested in their well-being at all. If we were truly interested in their well-being, why would we change our minds about them? Why would we get angry at them or do things to hurt them? It is because our loving-kindness is based on selfishness.

The fundamental problem is that our concern for the well-being of others is twisted by selfishness. There is no benefit from this kind of loving-kindness because it stems from an egoistic clinging motivated by self-interest. This loving-kindness will not benefit others, and it is not the same as a genuine interest in the well-being of others that has no connection with benefiting ourselves. We have to recognize this unstable loving-kindness, and we must begin to generate proper loving-kindness. The way to do this is to become less preoccupied with our selfishness.

We need to keep in mind that, just as we long for physical well-being, mental harmony, and peace, so do all other sentient beings, whether they are friends, enemies, family members, fellow citizens, animals, or whatever. All the activities people perform come from this desire for well-being. These include both beneficial activities as well as harmful and self-destructive activities which are based upon confusion and paranoia. Even when people perform harmful, self-destructive actions, they do so with the thought that such activities could make things better. Based on this understanding, we should be concerned for the well-being of others not because they are our friends or family members, or because they have done kind things for us or might in the future, but because we all share this fundamental situation. This is not based on any prejudice or bias, but is rooted in the reality of sentient beings' experience. If we come to terms with this understanding, how could we not be moved by concern for others' well-being? This genuine and heartfelt concern for the well-being of others is proper loving-kindness.

This kind of universal and unconditioned loving-kindness is something everyone can develop. Because of our tremendously powerful habit of self-interest and egoistic clinging, considering such an outlook might make us feel uncomfortable, but actually it is not difficult. We are talking about an attitude of mind, and to have an attitude or thought is not difficult at all. If you have a thought of loving-kindness that includes one being, you do not have to do anything extra to include all beings in that thought. On the other hand, if you think "I'm not able to have thoughts like that," you are just indulging in habitual ego-clinging. It is not true that you cannot have altruistic thoughts that include all beings. You have the freedom to have such thoughts at any time. Nobody can stop your mind! Because of the unobstructed nature of mind, there is no limit other than those that we impose.

We may wonder what the benefit is of having concern for the well-being of everyone. With this kind of attitude, our minds will be free from thoughts of envy or jealousy. Our usual notion of concern for others is just self-interest based on attachment, which leads to aversion, jealousy, and so forth. Even if we get rid of one object of jealousy, there will be another one, and another one after that. No matter where we go, and no matter what we do, jealousy will not go away.

However, when you are able to have a genuine outlook of loving-kindness, there is no jealousy because the thought of jealousy is removed. How so? Because there is no object of jealousy. If you have genuine interest in the well-being of everyone, there is no one to be jealous about. There is no one you *don't* want to have happiness and goodness. This idea is simple and very profound, and it is the opposite of our conventional approach, which makes such an outlook completely impossible. Unless we have a genuine and sane interest in the well-being of others, we will not be able to come out of our self-imprisonment and self-indulgence.

When you think about this idea, you should not just think, "Oh, maybe that's true." You should reflect on the fact that whenever we have a genuine thought of concern for the well-being of everyone, even if it is only for one moment, we cannot have a thought of jealousy at the same time. Having a thought of loving-kindness is in itself the purification of any jealous thought. It is not that we first have a thought of loving-kindness and then we get rid of jealousy, or that we first get rid of jealousy and then have the thought of loving-kindness in its place. We are not talking about material objects that we replace or move around, but about the quality of the thoughts that we introduce to our minds.

Most of the problems and suffering in our lives, whether local or global, personal or interpersonal, are caused by this pattern of jealousy. Wouldn't it be liberating and uplifting to be free of such a tendency? Even though we may understand that these patterns are harmful and want to be free of them, we still find ourselves constantly entrapped in them because of our deep involvement in our habitual mental patterns. And because we have accumulated these habits from beginningless time, we believe they are our inherent nature. In order to free ourselves from these difficulties, we have to first develop a proper understanding. Such patterns are not, in fact, our inherent nature.

Even though initially we are caught up in these patterns, we can acknowledge where we stand with respect to our potential for freedom, and we can develop a clear view of how to go about this process. Any small effort, any continuous attempt we make towards freeing ourselves from these habitual tendencies will amount to some definite, beneficial effect as long as our attempts are based on the right understanding, the right view, and the right approach. The right understanding is the practice of having concern for the well-being of all beings, again and again, and to see the wisdom of this. We do this practice not just because it is a nice thought, but because ultimately it is very profound and beneficial. Applying this understanding is the beginning of training the mind.

Therefore, in mahayana practice we emphasize the importance of training the mind with these Four Immeasurables. These are not just philosophical concepts; they must be incorporated into our lives. The more we train in the concern for the well-being of everyone, the more it becomes a heartfelt experience. That experience is so refreshing and such a source of spaciousness that we begin to feel our connection with the world and with others. When other beings come into view and we experience their happiness, it gladdens and inspires us. Because of our genuine concern for the well-being of others, it is a joyful experience to see others having a positive experience at any level. When we travel to other countries and see material prosperity and harmony among the people, our sense of friendship and affection increases because we relate to their well-being. We feel liberated instead of annoyed by their well-being because we do not have the conflicting tendencies of mind that usually come into play. Instead, we have genuine affection and friendship. And because of the connection between mind and body, we begin to physically feel a sense of space as opposed to feeling walled in, and nothing is more liberating.

Because of our strong habit of selfishness, we might think concern for the well-being of others leaves us out. This is not true, because concern for the well-being of others is in fact a source of great benefit to us. But we need to be careful; all along we have had tremendous concern for our own benefit, and this has been a source of harm. For this reason, repeatedly training our minds is important. Intellectual knowledge is not enough. Our habitual patterns predominate, and they will constantly challenge us; we can expect to have some difficulties working with our neurotic tendencies, but we need to persevere. Seemingly external problems are not as serious as self-created problems, and so this is where we should put most of our attention.

In the mahayana practice, we train ourselves in loving-kindness by repeating again and again words of aspiration. The prayer of aspiration of the Four Immeasurables begins:

May all sentient beings have happiness and the causes of happiness.

This refers to both relative and absolute well-being. "May all beings have happiness" refers to temporary well-being, and is the wish that people experience well-being wherever they are and whatever they are going through. "May all sentient beings have the causes of happiness" refers to accumulating and giving birth to the causes of happiness.

The causes of happiness are summed up by the three kinds of training. The first concerns body and speech, and the other two concern the mind. The first is proper discipline or conduct. This includes virtuous actions of body and speech, actions that are beneficial and contribute to the well-being of others. The second is training in samadhi or meditative stability and concentration. The Tibetan term for this is *ting nge dzin,* which means "freedom from fixated mind." It refers to the indestructible stability of mind which frees us from the distractions perpetuated by habitual tendencies. The third is training in wisdom. These three types of training result in freedom from confusion and suffering, which gives birth to happiness.

Sometimes these three types of training are referred to as the three disciplines: the discipline of proper conduct of body and speech, the discipline of stability of mind, and the discipline of wisdom and insight. Training in these three disciplines leads to accumulating and giving birth to the causes of well-being and happiness. You can experience this happiness and well-being right now, and in the future as well.

As long as we have proper understanding as well as a proper feel for the first immeasurable, loving-kindness, it is very easy to give birth to the second immeasurable, compassion. There is no essential difference between the two; it is just a matter of focus. The reason that immeasurable loving-kindness is introduced first is that if you are able to understand and cultivate this attitude and integrate this practice, then you will be able to do the others. If you are not able to understand and apply the first one, then you will not be able to understand and apply the rest. Therefore, the first immeasurable is extremely important.

COMPASSION

The second immeasurable is compassion. Here the focus is the pain and suffering of sentient beings. For us to apply this teaching clearly and properly, we must first understand what compassion is and why compassion is so profound and important.

Compassion means having a genuine aspiration for all beings to be free from suffering. The aspiration prayer of the Four Immeasurables states:

May all sentient beings be free from suffering and the causes of suffering.

First, we must understand what compassion is, and then we can understand limitless compassion. Limitless compassion has a quality of openness, accommodation, and spaciousness as opposed to territoriality and clinging. As in the case of loving-kindness, it is not that we do not ordinarily have compassion, but our normal view of compassion is twisted and confused. Because of our orientation toward "mine" and "me," we desire freedom from suffering only for those closest to us, and we have aversion for anyone not in this group. We also expect particular behavior or material things from the people closest to us, which makes our compassion suspect.

Limitless compassion, however, comes from the understanding that whatever beings may be going through and to whatever degree they may be confused, fundamentally, all of them long for freedom from pain and suffering just as we do. Understanding this basic situation, we also realize that the number of sentient beings is immeasurable. Because there are immeasurable sentient beings, immeasurable compassion is not limited to only some beings or one species of beings. There is no discrimination as to friends or foes, my group or other groups, but all beings, without exception, are included in limitless compassion. We cultivate this attitude towards all beings, wishing that they be free from suffering.

Suffering and pain are created by hatred and aggression and their various aspects—anger, resentment, rejection, grudges. All of these inflict suffering in our own lives or in the lives of others, both relatively and ultimately. While we are in a state of anger and hatred, we experience pain, and the consequences of our aggression will be a further experience of confusion, which leads to even more pain and suffering. By contrast, the attitude of compassion has no aggression or hatred and no intention to harm others. Again, there is actually no object of aggression and no object of hatred, if there is no one whom we want to see suffer.

Thus, this practice of compassion, particularly the practice of limitless compassion, is of tremendous benefit. It not only brings freedom from suffering and pain in the present, but also sows seeds for future freedom from suffering. To be able to integrate this will only come from true understanding, and we should therefore recognize the profundity of such understanding and practice. I should note that in the Buddhist teachings, by the way, when we say that something is profound, we are referring to how beneficial it is, not how fascinating or glamorous.

Normally, we believe that aggression is caused by external circumstances. We think that the object of aggression is "out there." However, we have no control over external circumstances. Also, no external circumstance is completely real or reliable because the nature of external circumstances is transitory, and also because all circumstances are interdependent. If we depend on external circumstances, thinking that by getting rid of one object of aggression we have somehow gotten rid of our aggression, in fact we have not. We can look to our lives for examples of this because this is what we have tried to do all along. We look outwardly and say to ourselves, "Here are the objects of hatred and aggression," and we try to destroy them. But have we become free of aggression and hatred? Have we become free of the suffering that results from such patterns of mind?

On the other hand, just as with loving-kindness, if you have a genuine experience of compassion with true understanding of what compassion is, there is no aggression. At the moment when your mind is filled with compassion, how can there be hatred? Having the attitude of limitless compassion is in itself the liberation of the opposing attitude of hatred and aggression.

When we speak of compassion, which is the wish that all beings without exception be free from suffering and the causes of suffering, it is important to know what suffering is. While there are many kinds of physical suffering, we classify all suffering into three categories: the suffering of suffering, the suffering of change, and all-pervasive suffering.

An example of the suffering of suffering would be when you are experiencing mental turmoil. Then on top of that, you feel physically sick. Another example is experiencing physical pain, and then experiencing mental confusion as well. This is the suffering of suffering: not only do we have pain, but in addition to the original pain, we experience even further suffering.

The second category is the suffering of change. In this case, being deceived by happiness is a cause of pain. Any sense of gain we experience will result in loss. Gain is deceptive because from the point of view of our conceptual fixation, our gain seems to be real, but from the perspective of the ultimate nature of things, it is not real or reliable at all. Change produces suffering because we believe that some illusion is the true, permanent reality. As a result, we are unable to accept change.

For example, when we experience fame, some honored position or recognition, we get excited and happy. However, if we fall from that position, then we experience suffering. If we did not experience fame, we would not have experienced suffering when it changed. Another example is becoming involved in a relationship which makes you very happy and joyful. However, when a separation occurs, this brings suffering, the suffering of change. This occurs because we viewed the relationship to be real and true, but it was not: it was a deceptive happiness that had the appearance of true happiness, but if it was really an experience of intrinsic happiness, it would not have changed. Such deceptive happiness is said to be the cause of the suffering of change.

The third type of suffering is all-pervasive, basic suffering. For example, when we are born, death is inevitable. All sentient beings are subject to the pain of death, and it cannot be avoided. As long as we are not liberated from basic confusion, which is composed of our conditioning and habitual tendencies, there will always be a basis for suffering. All-pervasive suffering is defined as the presence of this basic cause. As long as we have not experienced complete liberation, completely awakened mind, we will have these shortcomings and experience suffering.

In this prayer, we ask that beings be released from whatever mental and physical sufferings they are presently undergoing. As well, we consider not only their present suffering but all future suffering, so we ask that beings also become liberated from the causes of suffering. These causes are various habitual tendencies traditionally referred to as the three poisons: attachment, aggression, and ignorance. As long as there are these three tendencies or poisons of mind, there will always be suffering.

As long as we operate from a confused, negative outlook, an outlook based on attachment, aggression, or ignorance, our actions of body, speech, and mind are bound to produce suffering. Our body and speech are just tools at the disposal of our minds; whether they are harmful or beneficial depends on the motivation of the mind. If our mind is liberated from harmful and negative habits, our actions will also be free of harm to ourselves and others. Therefore, when we say, "May all sentient beings without exception be free from the suffering that they are presently experiencing and also be free from the causes of sufferings," we are asking that they be free from the various conflicting patterns of mind, and in particular the three poisons. With respect to these habitual tendencies, we need to keep in mind their harmfulness on a personal level as well as on an interpersonal level. In overcoming these tendencies, there would not only be liberation, peace, and harmony, but also an end to fear and suffering.

Therefore, limitless compassion is beneficial in helping us become free of all habitual patterns. In particular, it is the antidote for the conflicting patterns of hatred or aggression.

JOY

May all beings never be separated from the great happiness
that is free from all suffering.

The third immeasurable is supreme, unsurpassable joy. We are concerned not only with the immediate well-being of sentient beings, but we also have a vision for all beings to know the ultimate experience of awakened mind. From this point of view, the ultimate awakened mind experiences supreme, unsurpassable joy. We could have the attitude that not only may all sentient beings without exception experience happiness and be free from suffering, but may all beings also experience the absolute awakened mind.

Because that is our vision and motivation, we cannot be concerned with the temporary or relative happiness of beings. This is because relative happiness always carries the potential for more suffering, as we discussed in the context of the suffering of change. Therefore, we aspire that all beings experience the indestructible, ultimate awakened mind. This awakened mind is the wisdom which is the essence of unsurpassable joy, and we wish this for all beings without exception. We do not aspire for some beings to experience relative happiness and other beings to experience absolute happiness—we want all beings, without exception, to experience the completely awakened mind.

EQUANIMITY

The fourth immeasurable is immeasurable equanimity, which is the antidote for egoistic clinging and fixation. The fourth line of the prayer says:

May all sentient beings experience the state of equanimity
which is free from aversion and attachment.

Aversion and attachment come from egoistic clinging, and freedom from aversion and attachment is the experience of equanimity. We have already discussed the ego of self, which is the belief in and fixation on a self, on "me" and "mine." Then, there is the ego of others, the ego of phenomena, which is the belief in and fixation on other beings or objects, whatever seems to be outside of ourselves. We cling to the notion of self as well as to the notion of phenomena. If our minds are completely free from this dualistic fixation on self and others, then we will be able to have compassion and loving-kindness towards all beings equally.

In terms of the Four Immeasurables, this is the state of great equanimity. Such equanimity is the fruition of immeasurable loving-kindness, immeasurable compassion, and immeasurable joy. It is the ultimate and absolute experience of the awakened mind. Our practice should not be limited to developing temporary satisfaction, but should be dedicated to developing the ultimate experience of supreme, unsurpassable joy that is free from all conceptual notions of joy. The result of proper practice and proper view is this experience of immeasurable equanimity, which is free from aversion and attachment.

The Four Immeasurables are the very heart—the jewel and treasure—of the mahayana teachings. The Four Immeasurables are the reason this path is known as mahayana, the greater vehicle. It refers to greatness of heart and greatness of motivation, all-accommodating openness and great fearlessness. For beings like ourselves who are alive during these degenerate times, it is great fortune to have the opportunity to hear and work with such profound wisdom and to have access to such immeasurable value and benefit.

It is my sincerest hope that you will try to integrate these teachings into your lives, because the real experience, the real journey, lies in integration and understanding. If you train your minds in the Four Immeasurables, you are on the bodhisattva path and have introduced yourself to the bodhisattva family. The bodhisattva vow is very profound: it means stepping into the world of the bodhisattvas and proclaiming the truth of the development of your awakened mind.

However, such training is a challenge. It entails training in wisdom and developing a sharp, intelligent mind. For these reasons, proper understanding and application are essential. If there is no training of the mind—particularly if there is no understanding of or training in the Four Immeasurables—then you could take the bodhisattva vow hundreds of times and still miss the point. Even in the past, those who trained their minds properly achieved true realization of the teachings, but those who failed to train their minds, no matter how much they appeared to be involved in the teachings, were not able to achieve such realization.

As people living in the modern world, we have many duties and responsibilities. We are busy fulfilling various demands. As a result, we may have little time for formal Dharma practice. The question that arises again and again is: "How do we integrate the practice of Dharma into our everyday lives such that some quality of Dharma can manifest?" Wishing to do this and knowing how to do this are not enough. We must make some effort either through formal practice or through mindfulness. If we know exactly what to do but feel that we cannot carry out what we know, this is because there has not yet been a proper process of mind training.

The other important thing is that whatever amount of practice we are able to do—whether the formal practice of meditation or post-meditation practices such as virtuous actions of body, speech, and mind—we must do this practice properly. Quality of practice is the most important thing. If practice is done properly and if it is of good quality, then even a small amount can take us a long way. If it lacks quality and is not done properly, then even if it is done frequently, it may not amount to much. In this case, what I mean by properness and quality are in relation to the Four Immeasurables. When we perform any practice or virtuous action, it is important to remember to do it with the proper attitude: so all beings without exception can attain the completely awakened mind.

This aspiration for the mind of awakening is important because it is so possible to simply go through the motions of practice. How many people preface virtuous actions with this type of motivation? Knowing how few virtuous actions we do and how many unvirtuous actions and attitudes we indulge in, if we were to weigh these on a scale, the only thing that would tip the balance would be our motivation. Thus, we should incorporate the wisdom of this motivation whenever we practice or perform a virtuous action.

We should also work with motivation when we have completed an action or practice. This does not have to be an elaborate ritual, but just a simple dedication. We should have the sincere attitude that whatever benefit or virtue we have accumulated be dedicated to the relative as well as the ultimate benefit of all sentient beings without exception. We should not hold onto our action and say, "Oh yes, I did a good thing, so it is counted in my favor." Instead, we need to dedicate the merit, which is an application of the Four Immeasurables.

If you do dedicate the merit in this way, in time you will begin to experience the benefits of your action. However, any practice not joined by proper motivation takes a long time to produce any effect. In that case, our practice may also be tainted by neurotic tendencies and, as a result, we find ourselves involved in negative actions. Please try to keep this in mind.

QUESTIONS AND ANSWERS

STUDENT: Is it enough to practice loving-kindness in our minds if we are unable to practice it in the real world?

RINPOCHE: Training our minds with the attitude or habit of loving-kindness is important under any circumstances, whether we actually have the freedom to act in beneficial ways or not. We have to recognize that most of the time it is not that we do not have the freedom to perform beneficial actions, but instead that we lack the conviction and confidence to carry through such actions.

Typically, if there are convenient circumstances, we may feel inspired to momentarily engage in some good thoughts and actions. However, the moment the situation changes to something more adverse, we do not feel inclined to work with it. We always tend to attach some personal expectations, the wish for some sort of return. Such personal expectations may be obvious or they may be subtle. When those expectations are not met, we do not feel inclined to continue generating loving-kindness. And then, of course, we do not put it into action.

We may think to ourselves, "What's the point if it can't manifest outwardly?" However, the most important point is that if our minds are not properly trained, we will not have anything to communicate with confidence and conviction. We will only have things to communicate on the basis of impulse, which will be dependent on circumstances. And often, circumstances will not be favorable. But yes, generating such an attitude is in itself beneficial even if it is only an attitude. This is because this attitude eliminates contradictory motivations or thoughts. In the end, beneficial actions, skillfully and consistently performed, will come out of such training.

STUDENT: Did I understand you correctly to be saying that jealousy is the opposite of loving-kindness?

RINPOCHE: Unwholesome habits of mind give rise to further unwholesome habits, and wholesome habits of mind give rise to further wholesome habits. Among all the virtuous thoughts and practices, loving-kindness is the most direct way to diminish jealousy. If there is true loving-kindness and heartfelt concern for the well-being of others, then we will rejoice in their well-being, and this is the definite antidote for jealousy or envy.

STUDENT: There could be a group of individuals who are all sincerely working on their practice of loving-kindness, but they could have different styles. For instance, someone might be blunt rather than warm and sweet. Some people just don't like to talk a lot or wouldn't want to go up and hug somebody because it's not their style. Then there are some people who gush with friendliness and jump into your lap. Doesn't true loving-kindness have various manifestations?

RINPOCHE: What you said is helpful in clarifying a certain point, which is the difference between a genuine experience of loving-kindness and the pretentious imitation of it. In order to make a positive impression on others, some people want to appear glamorous or exciting. That would not be the approach of a practitioner who has genuine loving-kindness. It also does not mean that you need to react to things in an overly emotional way. You should have a deeply felt affection for others, with concern for their well-being. You know best what is true loving-kindness and what is deceptive loving-kindness. You are the best witness of your own progress or lack of progress because you know your mind better than anybody else. So yes, you have to recognize the difference between these two types of loving-kindness.

There are differences in the ways we manifest loving-kindness, but whatever our style, we should have the genuine experience of loving-kindness and not just know it intellectually. If you really have loving-kindness, then you will have heartfelt concern for whoever crosses your path. It is not an issue of an attitude such as, "Don't you know what I am doing for all you people?" That is not the point. You are working on your mind, developing concern for the well-being of everyone that you encounter. In that way, you touch everybody with your mind. When you see that people are happy and that they communicate well with each other, when there is friendship, physical health, and all the comforts of life, this is a cause for joy for us as well. Similarly, when you see that people are having success—spiritual, material, or whatever—you could think, "Good! How wonderful!"

This is a very intelligent thing to do. Some people think that we are only talking about creating good for others but, in fact, we also gain great benefit from such activity. This applies whether you say less or whether you say more, whether you are able to do a lot because you are skilled at doing certain things or whether you do less because you are not so skilled. Whatever we do we must do sincerely, although the degree and style may differ according to how much we have developed our loving-kindness, and according to the style with which we express that loving-kindness. Even though two people feel equally strong about the well-being of others, they could manifest this quite differently. There is also a definite flexibility in our minds and in our lives when we have cultivated the mind of loving-kindness such that we can be more fluid in our relations with others.

STUDENT: The economic, political, and psychological exchanges that occur outside this shrine room in the world around us operate on very different principles. I'm wondering how people who are attempting to practice this, as well as those who have achieved perfect loving-kindness can protect themselves from being abused in these exchanges.

RINPOCHE: First, it is important to refer back to the notion of recognizing that although there are differences in beliefs and value systems, all beings without exception equally yearn for happiness and freedom from suffering. Someone's belief might be completely contrary to yours because of that person's confusion, but he or she genuinely yearns for happiness and well-being. Fundamentally, there is no difference between you and them. It is very important that we understand this clearly, because the reason people abuse others is the result of not understanding other beings' fundamental problems and intentions.

If someone is involved in harmful and destructive activities, this is more harmful to the person participating in these activities than it is to those who are affected by them. For this reason, it is not appropriate to wish to hurt that person, although from the point of view of ego this is natural, as you well know. From the point of view of a wakeful mind, such an attitude shuts us off from potential wakefulness. The realities that people create are based on their egoistic tendencies.

You might have heard on a number of occasions that bodhisattvas have no enemies, and that whatever abuse we experience occurs because we have the conditions to attract that abuse. Also, we could never give birth to fearlessness if we were never subject to the abuse of others; without such experiences, your mind would not be open to the idea and the possibility of fearlessness.

What all of this really comes down to is that we need to train our minds. It is good that we are discussing these things, but I would like to emphasize that this discussion should not lead merely to further intellectualization, to going around and around with words. Your questions reflect some frustration due to lack of experience and lack of integration of the practice. Once you have some genuine experience of loving-kindness, not just a thought or intention, you will have a very different outlook about yourselves and the situations around you. On the more mundane level, you need to do the best you can do with your body and speech, and to work on training your mind.

In general, we want to control everything, but life does not work that way. Just do the best you can with respect to your intentions and actions. When there is a lack of confidence or conviction and you are discouraged about continuing, this is due to a lack of training. Being tireless and fearless is not just some kind of physical strength, but it comes from training your mind.

If there is definite danger coming your way, try to avoid being victimized to the best of your ability. If you are properly involved with the path, it would be wrong to take a position of animosity because that only creates further harm and confusion. However, you should certainly avoid being subject to harm in whatever way you can. You need to have a sense of discretion, and this is also emphasized in the teachings.

STUDENT: When you speak of integration, is the ease and ability to do this relative to karma?

RINPOCHE: Yes, very much so. It is an example of the truth of cause and effect. Even under ordinary circumstances, if we wish to train in a field with which we are already familiar, it will be easier than training in an unfamiliar field because we already have a foundation. Because we understand the language better, comprehension and communication are easier. In the practice of Dharma, if there is a better ground and foundation—a previous history of training your mind in loving-kindness and compassion, and a better history of virtuous actions of body, speech, and mind—then you will relate to Dharma as a familiar language, and you will be sharper and more sensitive.

We all have the potential to experience the awakened mind. However, we all have different propensities, and some can integrate Dharma more effectively than others. For instance, several people doing the same practice can put in the same amount of effort and energy, but they have different experiences because of the way they relate to the teachings. People who do not have a dharmic background or a history of virtuous action have the same potential, but if their habits have been counter to this potential and the means of developing it, then even the concept of immeasurable loving-kindness would not enter their language or strike a chord. That is why people hearing the same kind of teaching and doing the same kind of practice will understand them quite differently. People are different. Therefore, the history of your own karmic process will make a tremendous difference.

An Introduction
to the Bodhisattva Vow

As we have discussed, the first formal step on the Buddhist path is taking the refuge vows. Depending on the teacher and the student, the next step is usually taking the bodhisattva vow. It is essential to have a clear idea what the bodhisattva vow is, and how to prepare ourselves to take it. In this section, I will present an explanation of these points, and I will also try to share with you some of the history, inspiration, and indeed the preciousness of the bodhisattva vow. There are other explanations that will be given when you actually take the vow in person, such as how to maintain it purely as you put the bodhisattva path into practice.

TRANSMISSION OF THE VOW

The bodhisattva vow was transmitted by Shakyamuni Buddha, the enlightened Buddha, to the realized bodhisattvas Manjushri and Maitreya, who had achieved very high levels of realization. In turn, the bodhisattvas Manjushri and Maitreya transmitted the vow to Asanga and Nagarjuna, who were also highly realized. From that time up to the present day, this transmission has come down to us in a pure way from beings who have attained great realization.

The transmission that comes to us from Manjushri is known as *zabmo ta way gyu*, or "the lineage of the profound view." It was transmitted from Manjushri down to Nagarjuna, and from

Nagarjuna to Tilopa, Naropa, Marpa, Milarepa, and the Karmapas, all of whom had great realization. Because all the beings who held this transmission were highly realized, we say that this transmission is pure, immaculate, and splendid. When gold is melted and all the impurities are extracted, then the gold is pure. Likewise, the transmission of this vow, which has been passed down by realized beings to other realized beings, is a pure, immaculate transmission, and is therefore known as the "Golden Chain of the Lineage" or "the faultless, stainless, immaculate transmission."

In order to transmit this pure, immaculate bodhisattva vow, both the student and the teacher must have certain qualities. First, with respect to the teacher, he or she must have obtained the transmission from an authentic teacher. Second, that teacher must have kept the bodhisattva vow, not breaking it or giving it up. Third, the teacher should have the power of wisdom to give the transmission to the student. If the teacher lacks that power of wisdom, he or she will not be able to bestow the transmission. Lastly, having the previous three qualities, the teacher must have tremendous compassion, the altruistic intention to benefit living beings by giving the transmission. Love and compassion should be present within the heart of the teacher in order to properly give the vow.

As for the student, he or she should first have confident faith in the Buddha, Dharma, and Sangha. Without faith in the Buddha, Dharma, and Sangha, there is no ground to develop and cultivate bodhicitta. Thus, having faith, confidence, and trust is the first essential point.

Second, the student should long to receive the bodhisattva vow the way a sick person longs for medicine to heal his pain, or the way a thirsty person longs for water. If someone is not strongly motivated to obtain the bodhisattva vow, that person cannot cultivate bodhicitta. He or she is lacking the necessary will to do so.

Third, a person cannot appreciate bodhicitta if he or she does not know what bodhicitta is. By learning of the qualities and benefits of bodhicitta, we learn to appreciate and respect it, and then we will take bodhicitta seriously. The student should have appreciation for bodhicitta, the activities of great bodhisattvas, and of the mahayana tradition altogether, which means having respect for mahayana practice.

Finally, along with the earlier points—having confidence, having desire, and knowing the benefits and qualities of bodhicitta— our aspiration will be incomplete if we do not think of all sentient beings when we take the bodhisattva vow. The student should have the intention to liberate and benefit all sentient beings by means of performing practices of body, speech, and mind. We must cultivate the seed of wishing to liberate sentient beings from suffering so they can attain buddhahood. That intention must be present within the hearts of those who wish to receive the vow.

The qualities that are necessary for the teacher to give the transmission of the bodhisattva vow and the qualities that are necessary for the student to take the transmission are very rare in our present-day world. Personally, I do not have even a fraction of the four qualities that a teacher should have. Although I do not possess any of those good qualities, I do possess oral permission to bestow the bodhisattva vow from my guru, His Holiness the 16th Karmapa. Likewise, at this time in history, students may not strongly possess the necessary qualities that were just described.

This is a unique time in which we find ourselves. It is not a time to judge the quality of the student or the teacher. Instead, we must think about this on the basis of the Dharma itself. This means we should have trust in the teachings about the benefits of bodhicitta. We should have certainty in the benefit of taking the bodhisattva vow, and certainty that the transmission of the Dharma has been unbroken from the time of Shakyamuni Buddha until the present.

As we know, gold is very precious. If we are given gold and we know that this gold is completely pure, we do not really care who gives it to us. The giver is not important here. The important point is to know that we are getting pure, solid gold. In the same way, the main point about taking the bodhisattva vow is to know that the transmission is beneficial and pure. Therefore, one should take the vow simply believing in its purity and preciousness.

The Seven-Branch Prayer
Bodhicitta and Merit

I f we want to put pure liquid in a vessel, we must realize that the liquid will become tainted if the vessel is dirty inside. Therefore, we need to clean the vessel before we pour in the liquid. In the same way, what do we have to do to make ourselves perfect recipients of the precious transmission of bodhicitta? Two things are necessary: we have to get rid of whatever prevents us from developing ourselves, and we have to obtain that which gives us the capacity to develop ourselves.

The proper procedure for developing bodhicitta is just like planting a seed in the ground. When we plant a seed, it needs warmth, well-fertilized ground, and water. With these three things, the seed grows, the fruit develops, and its flowers bloom. Taking the bodhisattva vow from an authentic teacher is like giving a seed warmth, the accumulation of merit is like fertilizing the seed, and the development of compassion is like watering the seed.

Therefore, in order to cause bodhicitta to grow within ourselves, we first need to accumulate merit. Having accumulated merit, we must dedicate the merit with great compassion to all living beings, aspiring that they be liberated from the suffering of samsara, and wishing that they will experience the complete liberation of enlightenment. We have to understand that all the bodhisattvas in the past were able to attain the highest levels of realization through this same accumulation of profound, immeasurable merit.

A very profound way to accumulate this merit is to sincerely perform what is known as the Seven-Branch Prayer. It is called this because the prayer has seven parts or branches. The Seven-Branch Prayer is a prayer that is performed verbally in many practices and ceremonies, including before the Bodhisattva Vow ceremony. Some parts of it are also performed physically as an important part of Dharma practice, such as doing prostrations and making material offerings.

HOMAGE

The first of the seven parts is paying homage with your body, speech, and mind as a gesture of devotion to the buddhas and bodhisattvas. Paying homage with the body is often expressed by doing prostrations. (In fact, the same Tibetan word, *chag tsal,* is translated both as homage and prostration.). When we speak of the seven branches, paying homage is called the first branch. However, it is important to point out that paying homage is not really separate from the others. For instance, we traditionally pay homage verbally or prostrate physically before we make an offering, and indeed before the other branches as well.

MAKING OFFERINGS

The second of the seven branches is that of making offerings. Among the methods for making offerings are offering material objects, offering through mental means, and offering through physical means.

With respect to material offerings, if an individual is wealthy he or she can accumulate merit by making offerings to realized beings such as the Buddha. For example, a wealthy man who built numerous Buddhist monasteries and Buddhist study centers accumulated limitless merit and attained the state of a bodhisattva. In the same way, we can accumulate merit through making material offerings according to our own capacities.

If we cannot afford anything material, we can make mental offerings. For instance, we can imagine offering the whole universe, the sun, the moon, and so forth. In the Buddhist tradition we speak of Mount Meru, the four continents, the eight subcontinents, and the heavenly realms, and we can mentally offer all of these to the buddhas and bodhisattvas. We could also mentally fill all of space with beautiful flowers, and offer these to the buddhas and bodhisattvas. We do not cling to whatever precious objects our minds can imagine, but offer them one-pointedly to the bodhisattvas, and then we dedicate the merit to the benefit of all sentient beings. By performing such mental offerings, we accumulate merit, which is necessary in order to cultivate bodhicitta in ourselves.

You might think, "Since I am poor, perhaps I am unable to achieve the level of a bodhisattva." However, the ability to take the bodhisattva vow and achieve the level of a bodhisattva is not only for rich people. A person who is poor and unable to make material offerings can still take the bodhisattva vow and achieve the state of a bodhisattva simply by offering whatever he can afford and making mental offerings.

Long ago there was a beggar named Tathagata Ötro who took the bodhisattva vow from a buddha known as Tathagata Ö Thaye. He did not have any material objects to offer when taking the bodhisattva vow, so he burned some dry straw and imagined that he was burning incense and lamps. He offered with his imagination alone, and this was sufficient for him to attain the state of a bodhisattva.

Even if we are not in the position to offer even a little dried straw, we can still take the bodhisattva vow and attain the level of a bodhisattva by making the third type of offering, physical offerings. We can offer our physical bodies to the enlightened beings, not only in this life but for all future lives, asking that the enlightened beings give their blessings and power so our work and our bodies can help liberate sentient beings. For example, a man named Yonten Triden took the bodhisattva vow from the Buddha Nyingding. Since he was extremely poor and could not offer any material objects, he offered prostrations. By making this physical offering, he was able to take the bodhisattva vow and attain the level of a bodhisattva.

The reason we make these offerings is to please the enlightened beings. However, when we make these offerings, we are not actually able to satisfy these enlightened beings because they do not have any attachments. For an enlightened being, there is no difference between gold dust and common household dust because an enlightened being has gone beyond attachment. For enlightened beings there is no gold that is precious and no dust that is not precious. Therefore, when we offer a precious object such as gold, we cannot actually make highly realized beings happy, but we do accumulate merit for ourselves.

Since this is the case, how can we make enlightened beings happy? We can make them happy by practicing and accomplishing the authentic Dharma, and in that way benefiting living beings. The sole intention of the bodhisattvas is to benefit beings. Therefore, if we benefit beings, we please the enlightened ones. If we develop altruistic motivation, keep our bodhisattva vow commitment, practice the Dharma, and teach others how to practice, we will make enlightened beings happy and satisfied. Therefore, offerings of practice are very special and genuine in the path of Dharma.

Although Dharma practice is, in general, the one offering that pleases enlightened beings, the very best offering of all is to understand that phenomena have no inherent existence, that phenomena are not solid, real, or substantial. If we are able to come to a stable recognition of emptiness, we have moved from confusion to a state that is not confused. Our minds are no longer mistaken, and this is why we say understanding emptiness is the best offering.

CONFESSION

In order to take the bodhisattva vow, we have to confess all the negative actions or karma that we have accumulated in the past. We have committed many negative physical, mental, and verbal actions in all our lifetimes, and without making a confession we will remain impure, like a vessel with poison inside. Even if we were to fill such a vessel with pure substances, they would be mixed with the poison and become impure. Likewise, since we are the recipients of the vow, we are its vessel, and we must purify ourselves of negative karma through confession.

The source of all our misfortune, suffering, negative experiences, and adverse conditions is our negative actions and negative karma. Since no one wants to experience such suffering, we should admit that there is no real advantage to performing negative actions. Negative karma has no positive qualities; the only thing good we can say about negative karma is that if we confess our negative actions and regret them from the bottom of our hearts, they can be purified.

In order to make this confession, we need to apply what are known as the four powers of confession. The first power of confession is the object to whom you confess, and your faith in that object. You visualize limitless buddhas and bodhisattvas in the open space above and in front of you, completely covering the space in much the same way that a dense forest is covered with trees. Since the buddhas and bodhisattvas have achieved the state of omniscience and developed complete wisdom, it is possible to visualize them in that manner and invoke their presence from the pure realms. Having visualized the buddhas and bodhisattvas in this way, we feel true regret from the bottom of our hearts for whatever negative actions of body, speech, and mind we have performed, and we confess these negative actions to them.

The second power is acceptance, accepting the mistakes we have made. We performed negative actions of body, speech, and mind out of the defilements of attachment, anger, and ignorance. These activities were mistakes, and they led us to further experiences of suffering. The actions that we commit through negative thoughts are just like eating poisonous food: they lead us and other beings to experience more suffering and pain. Thus, accepting our negative actions and their results for what they are is the second power of confession.

It is quite difficult to remember the details of every negative action we have committed in this lifetime, let alone in previous lives. We do not need to remember everything precisely, we simply need to know that through attachment, anger, and ignorance we have accumulated limitless negative karma in our past lives and this present life. We should understand and accept our negative karma, and then confess it.

The third power of confession is to completely cut off negative karma by means of prayer and other purification practices. Perhaps the best known of these practices is the prayer known as the *Thirty-Five Buddhas* (it is also called the *Three Skandha Sutra*). In this prayer, we begin by reciting the names of thirty-five buddhas (beginning with Shakyamuni Buddha, the buddha of our time) and request these enlightened beings to purify us of negative karma, defilements, and obscurations. Just as we use detergent to remove a stain, we use this prayer to completely remove negative karma. If we apply this remedy correctly, then any negative karma we have accumulated can be purified by the blessings of the enlightened beings to whom we confess. If we believe in their presence and regret our negative actions from the depth of our hearts, there is no negative karma at all that cannot be purified.

For example, during the time of Shakyamuni Buddha, there was a person known as Sormö Trengwa, which roughly translated means "a garland of fingers." He earned this name in the following way: he met an unrealized teacher who, in order to misguide him, told him to kill one thousand human beings. Trusting this teacher, he went out and killed nine hundred and ninety-nine people. He was also told to make a finger from each of his victims into a garland and to wear it around his neck, and because of this he was called Garland of Fingers.

Needless to say, he was greatly feared, and everyone ran away from Garland of Fingers. As a result, he was unable to find anyone to kill in order to bring his total up to one thousand. He was so desperate he decided to kill his own mother. Buddha Shakyamuni was aware of this state of affairs through his omniscience, and he went to Garland of Fingers' home. When Garland of Fingers saw a monk outside his house he began to chase him, preferring to kill a monk rather than his own mother.

Through the Buddha's magic powers, the faster Garland of Fingers ran, the faster the Buddha went away, although the Buddha appeared to be walking very slowly. While they were walking, the Buddha was also giving teachings about negative karma and the results of actions. So, as Garland of Fingers chased the Buddha, he received these teachings. Not only was he unable to catch the Buddha, but eventually he realized all his negative actions and fell on the ground in regret. At that point, the Buddha turned around and accepted his confession. From then on, the regret felt by this man for his past negative actions was so powerful that he practiced with great diligence and concentration. He was not only able to purify the negative karma of killing nine hundred and ninety-nine people, but he achieved a high state of liberation in that very lifetime.

There is a similar story about a man named Day Gyay. Patricide and matricide are considered to be the most negative actions that a person can perform, along with killing a bodhisattva or one's spiritual teacher. Day Gyay had killed his own mother, and realizing that he had performed an immeasurable crime and not knowing what method to apply, he ran away from home. The idea of having accumulated this immeasurable negative karma haunted him constantly. He went from place to place, but could not find the correct method to get rid of his negative karma.

One day he was walking near a monastery and he heard the monks reciting a prayer that stated that all negative karma can be purified by means of confession. Hearing this, he felt tremendous relief, and he went to one of the monks and confessed his negative action. This monk taught him the correct method of confession and purification. Finally he had the right remedy. He practiced one-pointedly with regret and diligence, and again, he achieved spiritual liberation.

Then there is the story of a man who killed his own father, who was a fully ordained monk. The man was particularly uncomfortable because in addition to accumulating immeasurable bad karma by killing his own father, his crime was even greater because his father was a monk. However, because he was given the correct method of confession and because he applied this method, he also was able to achieve liberation.

No matter how much negative karma we have accumulated, if we apply the correct remedy and confess with genuine regret, that negative karma can be purified. This is like putting a small flame to a gigantic mountain of dry grass: the small flame can completely burn all the grass. Likewise, if we regret, confess, and apply the correct remedy, all the negative karma that we have accumulated in this life and in countless past lives can be purified and removed.

The fourth power of confession is the power of promising not to repeat the negative action. Suppose we ate poisonous food and got extremely sick, and a doctor helped us get the poison out of our system. Having experienced that, we would vow not to touch that poison again. Likewise, once we have confessed, we should have a strong intention not to repeat our negative actions.

This is the most difficult power of confession, and it is very important. The reason it is so important is illustrated by the following analogy. In order to grow a plant, we first need to cultivate the earth to make it ready. Then, we need to fertilize the land. With the help of the fertilizer, sufficient warmth, and regular care, the seed grows. However, if there is not a strong fence around the plant, there is a chance that wild animals may destroy it, so we must protect the plant by building a very strong fence. The fourth power is like the fence: by promising not to repeat negative actions in the future, we are building a fence, a protection around a growing seed.

If we apply the four powers, there is no negative karma that cannot be purified. So far, we have been unable to purify our negative karma because of ignorance. We did not know how to apply the four powers, or perhaps we did not take these powers seriously. However, all negative karma can be removed if we diligently apply the four powers.

REJOICING

The fourth branch is rejoicing. This means taking joy in the virtuous actions, success, and happiness of all living beings. When accomplished bodhisattvas perform compassionate actions, we rejoice at that. When a being at our own level enters into the bodhisattva path, we rejoice at this good action. We also rejoice at the actions of beings on the path of individual liberation (shravakas and pratyekabuddhas), as well as at the success, happiness, and well-being of ordinary living beings. Having rejoiced purely from our hearts, without jealousy, we accumulate as much merit as someone who has accumulated merit by practicing.

The following story illustrates how important it is to rejoice in the good actions of others. During the life of Shakyamuni Buddha, there was a wealthy and powerful king known as King Saljal. Because this king was extremely wealthy, he invited Shakyamuni Buddha to his house along with his thousands of attendants, and he requested that they perform a special practice. He provided them with food for forty-nine days, and this was the first time someone had hosted the Buddha along with his thousands of students for such a long period of time. There were also many beggars living outside the palace, waiting for leftover food from the gathering.

Toward the end of this practice, the Buddha was sitting on a high throne in the presence of his thousands of students as well as the king and queen, and was about to dedicate all the merit they had accumulated during the forty-nine days. The king thought, "Since I have accommodated the Buddha and his thousands of students, I am quite sure that the Buddha and his students will dedicate the merit first to me and then to my wife, the queen." The queen thought, "The Buddha and his attendants will dedicate all the merit either first to my husband and second to me, or perhaps I will be first and my husband second."

However, when the Buddha and the bodhisattvas actually dedicated the merit, they first named an old female beggar who was outside the gate, and only then the king, queen, and others. The king asked the Buddha why he did this, and the Buddha replied,

"While you were sponsoring me and my thousands of attendants during these forty-nine days, the old beggar outside was so moved by your actions that she rejoiced. She rejoiced at your good action, your ability to sponsor us, and prayed, 'May our King have such power in the future, and many, many more additional powers, to accommodate enlightened beings and their students.' Because she rejoiced in this way with a sincere heart, she accumulated greater merit than you, who accommodated us for forty-nine days. Because her heart was more pure, I dedicated it to her first." From this story, we can see that rejoicing is very powerful and important as a means for accumulating merit.

REQUESTING ENLIGHTENED BEINGS TO TURN THE WHEEL OF DHARMA

There are many buddhas and bodhisattvas throughout the universe who are not presently teaching the Dharma. This is partly due to the fact that beings lack interest in the Dharma and therefore we do not ask them to teach. For that reason, the fifth branch offering is to formally request enlightened beings to "turn the wheel of Dharma" (a term that refers to teaching the Dharma) for the benefit of all living beings. When we make this request, the buddhas and bodhisattvas hear us, and then they reveal the teachings. Because their teachings benefit limitless sentient beings, we accumulate merit by making such requests.

When Buddha Shakyamuni attained complete enlightenment, he remained in silence for 49 days, and during this time the god Brahma requested that he turn the wheel of Dharma for the benefit of living beings. Accepting this request, the Buddha revealed the profound teachings. Likewise, we must ask that enlightened beings turn the wheel of Dharma for the sake of all living beings suffering in samsara. Because of enlightened beings' omniscience and wisdom, they can hear us no matter how far away they are. If a person requests with a pure heart that a buddha turn the wheel of Dharma, the individual who requested the teachings will accumulate limitless merit as long as the teachings of that particular buddha continue to exist. In this way, requesting enlightened beings to turn the wheel of Dharma is a means to accumulate tremendous merit.

REQUESTING ENLIGHTENED BEINGS NOT TO PASS INTO NIRVANA

Because sentient beings need the teachings of enlightened beings and need to be liberated, we ask them not to "pass into nirvana." In Buddhist terminology, this particular phrase means to die or pass away, but in the particular sense of an enlightened being passing beyond samsara entirely and no longer relating to sentient beings. We ask that they remain with us until every single living being is enlightened. When we make this request, enlightened beings become aware that sentient beings need them, and they will stay on earth longer in order to benefit them. As we said before, highly realized beings can hear our prayers regardless of how far away they are. Then, as long as such teachers remain on earth and benefit beings, we will accumulate merit and will have the good fortune to have a teacher guide us on the right path. Therefore, the sixth branch is to request the teachers and enlightened beings not to pass into nirvana until all beings without exception are established in buddhahood.

If we make a fire and run out of wood, we go out to find some wood to add to the fire so it can continue to burn. Similarly, if we have an oil lamp that is about to go out because we are running out of oil, we will add more oil so the lamp can continue to burn. It is the same when we request the buddhas and bodhisattvas not to pass into nirvana, so they can continue to guide us with their profound teachings. We are praying to ensure that the flame of Dharma continues to burn.

DEDICATING THE MERIT

Whatever merit we have accumulated through doing prostrations, through making physical, mental, and material offerings, through confessing, rejoicing, and requesting enlightened beings to turn the wheel of Dharma and not pass into nirvana, we dedicate the merit of this to all sentient beings, wishing that they reach enlightenment. Because of that dedication, because you do not take or cling to this merit as your own, as "mine," the merit becomes inexhaustible.

Having performed these seven branches, we have all the qualities needed to obtain the teachings and practice the Dharma. We have accumulated merit, and we have been purified by applying the four powers of confession. Therefore, we have become perfect vessels to obtain the Dharma. For this reason, this prayer is often done in preparation for the bodhisattva vow.

QUESTIONS AND ANSWERS

STUDENT: Concerning the fourth power of confession, should we promise to abandon just our negative actions or should we also promise to abandon the ignorance and mental afflictions that cause them?

RINPOCHE: We should keep in mind that our spiritual growth takes time. We should not expect to become stainless, perfect people overnight. When you cultivate plants, they take time to grow; it takes time for flowers to blossom and then produce fruit. Similarly, when we hear about the good qualities that occur at the higher stages, we may want them so much that we expect to achieve results overnight. However, this is not possible.

With respect to taking the fourth vow not to repeat negative actions, the reason we say actions and not emotions is to help us be mindful not to accumulate negative karma in the future. Because we have not completely developed ourselves and are still ordinary people, we continue to have defilements such as anger, hatred, jealousy, pride, and so forth. Although we have made a commitment not to act negatively in the future, we still have neuroses and defilements. Beginners on the path are bound to develop anger, hatred, and jealousy, which all lead to the accumulation of negative karma.

The fourth power, making the commitment not to repeat negative actions in the future, is helpful as a reminder. It is like saying to ourselves, "Oh, I have taken the vow not to repeat negative actions." The moment we develop neurotic feelings and negative emotions, we remember this vow and this prevents us from actually performing the actions. In this manner, we gradually eliminate the defilements in our minds. This fourth power is somewhat like a defense, a reminder that keeps us from performing negative actions. However, it is important to remember that as beginners it is very natural for these defilements to arise in our mind.

When we start the practice of bodhicitta and the path of spirituality, we have to act and proceed as beginners. There are many skillful means to purify ourselves from negative actions of body, speech, and mind, and one of the most effective is the daily confession prayer. Since we are beginners, we accidentally break the vow many times per day and so we recite the confession prayer every day. This way we keep ourselves from impurities and making ourselves pure again.

When you wear a new shirt, it is impossible to keep it clean. So you wash it, and then you can wear it again. In the same way, at the beginning of our path we accumulate negative karma that needs to be purified on a daily basis, and so we have to confess every day.

STUDENT: In asking buddhas to turn the wheel of the Dharma, is it to teach others or to teach me so that I can eventually teach others?

RINPOCHE: You ask enlightened beings to turn the wheel of Dharma for the benefit of all living beings, and this is for you as well as others. However, when you are a realized being, you do this strictly for the benefit of other beings. In the situation that I mentioned, after Shakyamuni Buddha reached enlightenment, Brahma made the request because at that time there were no other living beings who knew how to pray and properly request for the wheel of Dharma to be turned. Therefore, Brahma did so for the benefit of living beings. Because of this, Shakyamuni Buddha turned the wheel of Dharma. As a result of Brahma's request, the teachings are still available to us now. If you ask both on your own behalf as well as for the benefit of all beings, this indicates that you are at the ordinary stage of development.

STUDENT: I would like to have more explanation about the buddhas and bodhisattvas who are not turning the Dharma wheel, and how we go about requesting that. What do we actually do?

RINPOCHE: The method for requesting that the buddhas and bodhisattvas of the ten directions turn the wheel of Dharma is really mental; it is a prayer. We mentally ask the buddhas and bodhisattvas of the ten directions to turn the wheel of Dharma according to the capabilities of each and every living being. Generating this wish with our minds and then saying the words makes it a request. A person who requests in such a manner, with a really sincere heart, accumulates a lot of merit.

Because of an individual's accumulation of merit, that individual as well as other sentient beings will mature karmically and will be able to receive the teachings. The buddhas and bodhisattvas who are not turning the wheel of Dharma are waiting for sentient beings to mature. When sentient beings are mature enough to accept the teachings, then those beings turn the wheel. To develop ourselves and other sentient beings, we request in the form of a prayer.

The Six Perfections

We have discussed the idea of bodhicitta quite a bit so far, and in the last chapter we talked about the bodhisattva vow, which is the transmission of the formal commitment to take up and practice bodhicitta. Therefore, at this point, it would be good to summarize exactly what is meant by this essential term in a concise way. Bodhicitta has two aspects, relative and absolute. Absolute bodhicitta is the pure enlightened mind itself. We have talked about it in terms of the wisdom that arises from vipasyana, but you should understand that this wisdom is uncreated, in the sense that it abides inherently as the essence of the mind of all beings. The journey to enlightenment is the process of recognizing this absolute bodhicitta. That is where relative bodhicitta comes in. Relative bodhicitta is what makes it possible to realize absolute bodhicitta.

Relative bodhicitta also has two aspects, and the first of these is called aspiration bodhicitta. We have seen how the impartial attitude of compassion to all beings is essential to the mahayana Buddhist approach. In fact, aspiration bodhicitta goes beyond just having compassion for all beings. It is the mental attitude of genuinely wanting not only to benefit and help sentient beings, but to establish them in full enlightenment, which is the ultimate and permanent benefit. It means having such a wish regularly and consistently, not just once or twice. Of course, just wishing or aspiring to bring beings to enlightenment, important as it is, is not enough. We need to actually make it happen. The practice of benefiting others and bringing them (and ourselves) to enlightenment is the second aspect of relative bodhicitta. It is called implementation bodhicitta because it is the actual implementation of the path. In taking the bodhisattva vow, we not only commit to the inner attitude of aspiration bodhicitta, but also to benefiting beings by putting implementation bodhicitta into practice. How does a bodhisattva practice implementation bodhicitta? By practicing the Six Perfections.

Since it is the very method used to accomplish enlightenment, we can regard these six perfections, (*paramitas* in Sanskrit) as the essential practice of Mahayana Buddhism. I would like to make it clear from the beginning that these six perfections are not something we acquire outside ourselves, but something we already possess within.

THE PERFECTION OF GENEROSITY

The first of the six perfections is the perfection of generosity. This, of course, means giving. Generosity is divided into four categories: material generosity, dharmic generosity, giving protection from fear, and the generosity of loving-kindness. Material generosity is connected to body; dharmic generosity is connected to speech; giving the protection of fearlessness is an act of body, speech, and mind; and the generosity of loving-kindness is based on mind.

MATERIAL GENEROSITY

We have to be clear that when we perform an act of material generosity, whatever we give will be used skillfully. For example, to kill an animal to feed a starving person is mistaken generosity, as is giving someone poison to kill himself or someone else. Therefore, before performing an act of material generosity, we must be careful that whatever is given is used beneficially and will not harm other beings. Check carefully as to how your material generosity will be used; if a person is really in need, then we should give according to our capacity.

There is a difference between worldly generosity and generosity according to bodhisattvas. In the case of worldly generosity, we may well be giving to remove pain, poverty, starvation, and illness. However, because we are in the world, we have the tendency to expect something in return. Either we give something to a person so they will do what we want, or we are generous in the hope that people will praise our kindness. Sometimes we give out of a sense of competition: "Since she gave so much, I should give a little bit more." Finally, we sometimes give with the thought, "Maybe if I give this and accumulate merit, I will take a better birth in the next lifetime." Generosity performed with such intentions is worldly generosity.

With respect to generosity as performed by a bodhisattva, although they still give material things, it is very different because there is no expectation of receiving anything in return. Of course, the bodhisattva performs acts of generosity with care, but there is no expectation of gaining fame or a better future birth. In addition, bodhisattvas dedicate the merit of virtuous actions to the benefit of all living beings and therefore there is no attachment to that deed. That is why the bodhisattva way of performing generosity is superior, and leads to a greater accumulation of merit.

DHARMIC GENEROSITY

The second generosity is dharmic generosity. Regarding this type of generosity, a person should first practice well to reach a level where they have the capacity to teach others. Once someone has reached this level, they should always be ready to give teachings. Whether they are surrounded by many students or just a few, they should teach in a happy and peaceful state of mind, and therefore set a positive example. Most importantly, when giving teachings they should maintain the bodhisattva view, which is to have compassion for all living beings. They hope that every word they speak will be helpful to all living beings and that, even by hearing one word, the seed of enlightenment may be cultivated in each student.

As beginners, you may be discouraged to hear that, in order to practice dharmic generosity, one must first obtain the ability to teach others. You might think, "Well, if that's the case, then I cannot perform dharmic generosity at all." However, do not get discouraged. There are many ways to perform dharmic generosity, not only through teaching. For instance, spending your time, effort, and money to come to teachings is itself dharmic generosity, because by doing so you have also made it possible for others to listen to the teachings.

A good example of this concerns a student of mine in Venezuela. When we first met, it was difficult for her to even think of setting up a Dharma center. However, she wanted to make Dharma available so people could join in the practice and learn how to remove their confusion. She decided to try her best. At first, it seemed she was the only Buddhist in all of Venezuela. One day, she went to a fashion show, and the man who was putting on the fashion show had a blessing cord[6] around his neck. She talked to him immediately after the show and discovered that he was a Buddhist: he had taken refuge and studied Buddhism in Dharamsala, India. They hugged each other and cried for a long time, feeling connected in the belief that they were the only people in that town practicing Buddhism.

The two of them worked very hard, and eventually they attracted about 300 students. After about three years they were able to invite me, and now I have been there three times. Although these 300 students do not live together, they live quite near each other and meet regularly. They were also able to establish centers in other towns, bringing the total number of students to about 500. Thus, even though you may not have the ability to teach, you can still make this precious Dharma available, and that is dharmic generosity. Since then, these two have established a formal center and are inviting teachers from all over the world. This is another example of dharmic generosity.

From this story, we can see that just through the efforts of a few people, many people have been given the opportunity to study the sacred Dharma. If we think clearly about this, making Dharma available is a far better way to perform dharmic generosity than trying to teach Dharma before you are qualified to do so.

---

6   A red cord that lamas give as a blessing.

THE GENEROSITY OF GIVING
THE PROTECTION OF FEARLESSNESS

Next, there is the generosity of giving protection from fear. Giving protection to those in physical danger is the most direct example of this kind of generosity. It could also include giving advice to those who seek it, and in a more indirect way, providing food or clothing is also giving the protection from fear. By helping people feel supported and cared for, we are doing more than just giving them physical goods. Whenever we are able to free beings from fear, we are practicing this kind of generosity.

THE GENEROSITY OF LOVING-KINDNESS

Finally, there is the generosity of loving-kindness. You might think that loving-kindness is a state of mind developed through meditation practice, and therefore wonder, "How do we perform such generosity of loving-kindness?" Well, when you love someone, then your every act of body, speech, and mind is very sincere. Along with that, we can relate our problems more easily to a loving, caring person than to someone who is not very caring, and does not listen to us. The more loving and caring we are, the easier it is for others to tell us their problems and fears. Knowing their problems, we can help according to our capabilities. Therefore, this generosity of loving-kindness is also necessary in the performance of the generosity of body, speech, and mind.

When we are sincere, open, caring, and loving, we do not need to search for people to receive our generosity. As long as we have the motivation of wishing to perform pure generosity, opportunities will present themselves. The perfection of generosity is performed with a pure attitude, with no expectation of receiving anything in return, and always with the wish that your actions will help other beings. That is real, perfect generosity.

Perfect generosity can be literally translated as "generosity gone beyond." Paramita is a Sanskrit word that means "transcendental" or "gone beyond." There can also be generosity that is not perfect, not paramita, which simply involves being good or kind.

However, the paramita of generosity is to give something with complete bodhisattva mind.

Performing perfect generosity should not be understood to mean that we should give and give until we become penniless. It means giving appropriately and with a proper attitude.

THE PERFECTION OF MORALITY

The second perfection is the perfection of morality, which is divided into three categories: renouncing negative actions, accumulating virtuous actions, and benefiting living beings.

Renouncing negative actions means that in order to help others, we have to first purify ourselves. For example, we wash our hands before we help someone else clean up. Similarly, in order to help others, we have to abandon all negative actions. Having abandoned negative actions, we then need to cultivate virtuous actions. However, renouncing negative actions and accumulating virtuous actions for the benefit of ourselves alone, or because we are forced to do so by someone else, is not considered morality. Neither is keeping pure morality in hope of gaining fame and praise. If we keep pure moral conduct for the benefit of all living beings, this is perfect moral conduct. Otherwise, if there is any notion of self-interest within this practice, it is not perfect morality according to the higher path.

Take the example of a shepherd. Early each morning, the shepherd takes the sheep to the mountains, where there is fresh grass. Now, the shepherd does not go there to eat grass! The shepherd is thinking of the well-being of the sheep. On the mountain, the shepherd cannot just fall asleep, but must constantly watch the sheep, making sure they are safe and that there are no wolves around. In the evening, the shepherd brings them home. This process goes on every day.

That kind of motivation, thinking only of the welfare of others, is necessary when practicing any of the paramitas. It is especially important in renouncing unvirtuous actions and practicing virtuous actions. You should always think that whatever you are doing is for the benefit of others, not just for yourself.

THE PERFECTION OF PATIENCE

The third perfection is the perfection of patience. The term can also mean "tolerance," because it really means going beyond anger or aversion in any situation. The perfection of patience is also divided into three categories. The first of these is not getting angry, and not retaliating, when others offend or harm us. It means remaining in a state of compassion and loving-kindness, no matter what. As beginners, and especially in the case of some sort of severe harm, this is difficult to do. We are not expected, as beginners, to willingly bring upon ourselves any sort of harm or abuse, but certainly major and minor situations will come up, just in the course of life events, where we could become angry. To remain calm and avoid angry reactions in such situations is this practice of patience. The training in tonglen practice becomes very valuable in practicing this kind of patience

The second category is having patience with Dharma practice and developing certainty in it. When we practice Dharma we have to face a lot of challenges, and we experience many ups and downs. Although we may go through tremendous obstacles and difficulties, we should have patience, developing the certainty that practice will bring results. We should think that whatever pain we go through is for the benefit of all living beings as limitless as the sky, and not for ourselves alone. If we have that attitude, then we have developed the patience of developing certainty in the Dharma.

This type of patience involves not getting discouraged when we encounter conflicts and hindrances. As practitioners, we meet different sorts of people with various ideas. Some might say that what we believe is wrong, and that the time and energy we spend practicing is a waste. We should not get discouraged about such conflicts. We should understand that because the other person does not understand Buddhism, he or she may not accept what we are doing. We should develop compassion for the person's lack of knowledge, and continue following our path with the hope of being able to benefit others. Of course, we may have to face greater difficulties, but this is just an example that comes to mind.

We have to first get used to the practice of loving-kindness and compassion in order to do well with the practice of patience. We should keep to the practice of loving-kindness and compassion and not explode with anger and frustration, and this will help us develop patience.

The third kind of patience or tolerance is more subtle or advanced. It means to have tolerance or acceptance for the profound nature of reality that is beyond what we ordinarily experience or think about. In some cases, people may reject or not even take seriously the deep and precise explanations about the nature of reality that are given in the Dharma. They don't really understand it, either conceptually or in terms of actual experience, and they back away from having openness toward it. Obviously, that is a serious obstacle to spiritual progress. In some sense, the third kind of patience is fearlessness toward understanding and experiencing ultimate reality which, for us, is new and unfamiliar. Because this kind of tolerance allows us to progress in a very profound way, it is very important.

THE PERFECTION OF DILIGENCE

The next perfection is diligence, which means to have great joy, interest, and willingness to practice virtuous actions. As beginners, we do not have very much motivation toward the practice of Dharma. As a result, we are not able to devote ourselves completely. It is necessary to develop the strong motivation that brings diligence. Generally speaking, lack of diligence indicates that someone does not really understand the point of Dharma and the future benefits of practice. If someone knows what the future benefits are, they develop diligence spontaneously.

One aspect of diligence is consistency. Diligence is needed not for a day or two, but on a consistent basis. Whatever time we have set aside for our practice and meditation should be kept regularly. Such effort gradually leads us to develop joy in the practice. We begin to experience the consistency of diligence as part of ourselves and, eventually, it becomes effortless. Although we talk about diligence as one among the six perfections, we actually need to apply diligence in the practice of each of the perfections.

Another aspect of diligence is called the diligence of applying devotion. This kind of diligence is basically a remedy for laziness. Applying devotion means that when we are practicing, we do not hesitate to practice, and we are not overcome by laziness. For example, you may have a regular practice of doing 100 prostrations a day. However, on a particular day you may not feel like doing 100 prostrations. Not letting this laziness rule you, you do 200 instead. If your mind keeps saying, "No, I can't do 200," then do 400. This is the diligence of applying devotion. If you practice in this way, you will overcome laziness and not pull back from practice. Otherwise, if you feel lazy one day, you will not practice, and if you feel lazy the next day, you will not practice again, and that pattern continues.

I would like to tell you a story about a Kadampa[7] monk, but first I have to tell you about *tsampa*, which is a nutritious Tibetan food made from barley flour. Traditionally, it is carried in a sturdy container, usually made from expensive fabric. The Kadampa monk said that when you perform generosity, if you have only one bag of tsampa and feel hesitant to give half of the tsampa to the poor, "Do not feel hesitant. Give not only half of what is in the bag, but even the bag itself!" That is a Kadampa bodhisattva practice for overcoming hesitation.

THE PERFECTION OF MEDITATIVE CONCENTRATION

The fifth perfection is called meditative concentration. Building meditative concentration begins with shamata practice. There are two types of meditative concentration: worldly meditative concentration and meditative concentration beyond the worldly level.

Worldly shamata meditation builds meditative concentration for the practitioner, and brings a strong sense of mental peacefulness. People tend to cling to that peacefulness, become attached to it, and work to acquire even more of it. As a result of clinging to this

---

7   A follower of the Kadam school, one of the important early schools of Buddhism in Tibet.

peacefulness, they may obtain meditative concentration. However, this does not lead to complete liberation because they had been aiming only for their own benefit, and they become attached to that experience. With that attachment to tranquility, they remain in the wheel of samsara.

With meditative concentration that goes beyond the worldly level, we aim to pacify our minds and remove our neuroses so we can help others do the same and thereby relieve their suffering. It is this motivation that takes shamata beyond the worldly level.

THE PERFECTION OF WISDOM

The sixth perfection is the perfection of wisdom. This perfection is divided into three parts: the wisdom of hearing, of contemplation, and of meditation. We can say that the perfection of wisdom develops as a result of our previous practice of the first five perfections. From another perspective, the perfection of wisdom needs to be a part of the other five perfections because it forms a basis for how these practices should be performed. In other words, all of the first five perfections need to be performed with wisdom for them to be truly transcendental. In that way, all six perfections work together.

THE WISDOM OF HEARING

We cannot practice without first listening to the teachings. As with any subject, we must first learn about it. For example, with respect to the six perfections, we must first learn the correct methods for performing the perfections, and we do this by hearing. Hearing can come from listening to teachings in person from authentic teachers, and it can also involve reading texts and other ways of studying.

THE WISDOM OF CONTEMPLATION

In addition to hearing and absorbing what we have been taught, we must try to familiarize ourselves with it, and make it part of ourselves. We should think the teachings over carefully, and consider whether they are valid, using our own independent intellect. Asking questions and discussing the teachings is also part of this.

By applying contemplation, we will gain true confidence about the teachings and whatever methods we are following.

THE WISDOM OF MEDITATION

When we have gained understanding and confidence through hearing and contemplation, the third step is meditation. Without the first two steps, we cannot really enter into practice, because if we do not know the method and are not certain about what we are doing, we cannot effectively meditate. But if we build upon learning and contemplation, it is possible to practice.

Gaining meditative experience is more profound than hearing and contemplation. If you gain meditative experience, you become a master of what you have learned. Having applied the wisdom of listening and contemplation, you then realize fundamental wisdom through meditation. Fundamental wisdom means to realize that everything we have experienced in our lives—pain, frustration, difficulties, fear, and so forth—could be transformed into wisdom. We know the methods for doing this, and realize that we have within ourselves all that we need in order to transform our pain and neuroses into wisdom. As well, we realize that the sacred buddha nature is within ourselves. Through our diligence in practice, we are able to transform those neuroses into wisdom, just like a flower blossoming. We gain this awareness, this fundamental wisdom, from the foundation of the wisdoms of listening and contemplation.

Having established the fundamental wisdom, next comes what we call path wisdom. With path wisdom, we develop complete certainty in the results of practice, with no doubts left in our minds. It is similar to the way that, when we first practice sitting meditation, after a certain period of time we develop peacefulness and understand that it is possible to develop even further tranquility. Then we feel more relaxed and sure about our meditation. From that slight sense of peace, we develop clarity and establish a very lasting peace of mind. What was just a feeling at the beginning later becomes an experience, which is established in your mind. When such peacefulness is established, we gradually come to understand the extent to which our anger and jealousy have decreased. We see these results for ourselves. Having seen such results, we develop one hundred percent confidence.

If someone explains how to make a fire by rubbing together two sticks of wood, and we do nothing but simply place them together and watch them, we will obviously never see a fire. However, if we rub the two pieces of wood rapidly together, we will first get some smoke. If we continue to rub them, we will see sparks flying. If we continue to rub them together energetically, we will eventually have a fire. Just as this persistent effort lets us start a fire, if we put persistent effort into the path of practice, it will lead us to the realization of wisdom.

THE FIRST BHUMI

Through diligence in the path of wisdom, we can come to the realization of absolute bodhicitta. This is equivalent to the first bhumi, the first stage of enlightenment. At that level, nothing can interfere with your experience, and nothing can put doubt in your mind because your mind has been cleared. It's like when you eat candy; you know from experience that it is sweet. If someone says it is bitter, you do not believe it because your experience tells you otherwise. Similarly, at this level of wisdom, no matter how many people try to make you change your mind, no matter how many beings try to make you stir up your mental afflictions, they can do nothing. Your mind has become clear and certain.

A practitioner reaches the first bhumi by applying these six perfections. After reaching this first stage, that person can then perform the perfection of generosity in its true meaning, which has four categories.

The first is that their generosity is performed with caring, gentleness, and no expectation of receiving anything in return.

Second, any advice is given gently, with much care and consideration.

Third, all activities are performed without pride, without ego. Any communication or action is given according to whether the other person is interested or not. If there is interest, the bodhisattva gives that which will help the other person.

Fourth, the bodhisattva reveals the Dharma. At this level, someone has developed the ability to teach. Those who have attained the first level of enlightenment do not brag about their achievements, and they do not consider themselves to be some sort of higher being. Instead, they praise others with great gentleness, and reveal teachings that are suitable for each person individually. In that way, the bodhisattva reveals the teachings gently and with modesty.

QUESTIONS AND ANSWERS

STUDENT: What do you mean by wisdom? We have heard this word so many times, but I would like to know what your definition is.

RINPOCHE: Wisdom in Tibetan is sherap. SHE (pronounced SHAY) means knowing and it refers to knowing every phenomenon or object as it is, knowing everything without mistake. RAP means excellent, higher, or correct. Putting these meanings together, the term sherap means excellent or higher knowledge. It is really a synonym for vipasyana or insight, since it refers to an insight, a direct knowing, of the nature of absolute reality. Sherap also refers to the extraordinary knowledge that spiritually awakened beings have, such as knowledge of the past and future, of past lives, and so on.

STUDENT: What is the meaning of the union of means and wisdom? I read about this all the time, but it just doesn't click.

RINPOCHE: If you have developed limitless compassion as well as the wisdom that knows the outer and inner needs of a person, you are also able to apply skillful means with the help of such wisdom. Knowing not only the outer needs of a person but also their true inner needs, you can apply skillful means to remove the root of that person's suffering. That is why it is called applying skillful means with wisdom.

STUDENT: How do we obtain wisdom?

RINPOCHE: We can divide wisdom into two categories: ordinary or worldly wisdom, and extraordinary or supreme wisdom, which is wisdom beyond the world. Worldly wisdom can be obtained in many different ways, such as going to school. Learning about the world is ordinary wisdom; it is knowledge that we did not have before, knowledge that we obtain or develop. Along with study or instruction, many kinds of worldly wisdom, such as mastering an art or a professional skill, require some kind of practice. The wisdom that is beyond the world is obtained in an analogous way to worldly wisdom. We study Dharma and spirituality, and we not only study it, we practice it. Through practicing, we develop that wisdom.

STUDENT: My question is about compassion, anger, and skillful means. If a student is ignorant and very stubborn in this ignorance, out of compassion, the teacher could become very angry and threaten the student. This frightens the student, so is this true skillful means or a mistake?

RINPOCHE: What do you think?

STUDENT: I don't know. I have doubts.

RINPOCHE: OK, let me ask you a question, which is of course a question for everyone. What if you change the people in your example to a mother and child? The mother is very compassionate and the child is like the student that you described. What do you think about that? Could it be skillful for a parent to get angry?

STUDENT: Definitely—I want to show my son how important something is!

RINPOCHE: When we apply skillful means and compassion, we have to see the ultimate results of our actions. We should be clear that compassion does not mean spoiling someone. Out of compassion, we might want to discipline the child, the student, or whoever it may be. If that discipline will ultimately lead them to happiness, then at that moment it is not considered to be uncompassionate. It is a compassionate act because of the ultimate purpose.

For example, if you have sick pet, such as a dog or cat, and it refuses to take its medicine, sometimes you simply have to open the pet's mouth and stick the pill in. On the other hand, you could act in ways that are extremely gentle physically and seem to be quite caring. But are you really creating the needed benefit? If not, that is not compassionate action. Whether an action is compassionate or not really depends upon whether your motive is to benefit others or not.

STUDENT: In developing the six perfections, is the practice to develop them one at a time or to work on them all simultaneously in a general way?

RINPOCHE: They are all practiced together. You first perfect the first and second perfections, which are the somewhat grosser ones. Then later you practice the subtler ones. It is like holding six threads of different lengths, keeping them together and then pulling on them. When you do this, the shorter threads come through first, and you still hold onto the longer ones until they are gone. Likewise, we practice the perfections together, but we perfect the gross aspects of practice before the more subtle ones.

At a deeper level, each perfection contains or embodies all the others. I spoke earlier about how diligence needs to be applied to the other five perfections. To give an example of how one perfection contains all the others, let's consider the first, generosity. When you practice the perfection of generosity, you are performing all six perfections. First, whatever you are giving is the generosity of giving. And if you give carefully, with a peaceful mind, this is performing generosity with perfect morality, the second perfection. You will not always be thanked for giving in this way; you may even be taken advantage of, criticized, or humiliated. Not losing your temper but continuing to give with loving-kindness and care is performing generosity with perfect patience, the third perfection. By giving with enjoyment and always looking forward to helping others with interest, openness, and enthusiasm, you are performing generosity with the fourth perfection, diligence.

Sometimes we get distracted when we are giving; for instance, if we become distracted when pouring a cup of tea, we will spill it. You need to concentrate on the cup, the amount of tea, and when to stop. By giving any object with precision and mindfulness, you give while maintaining the fifth perfection, the perfection of meditation. And knowing how to give generously, knowing the result of such generosity, and dedicating the merit of such generosity, are all wisdom, the sixth perfection. Thus, if your mind and heart are one-pointed, you practice all six perfections at once.

STUDENT: What is the correct attitude for dedicating merit?

RINPOCHE: As long as you hold three points in mind, you will practice and dedicate the merit skillfully. The three points are: one, at the beginning of your practice, think that the purpose of your practice is to benefit all living beings. Second, in the midst of your practice, whether it is visualizations or something else, remember that what you are doing is done only for the benefit of others. Finally, at the conclusion of practice, dedicate all the merit for the cultivation of buddhahood in every living being. As long as you keep these three points in mind, you will skillfully follow the mahayana path and will have no difficulty going towards the vajrayana path.

Dedicating the merit is essential because you make that merit inexhaustible, even if you have accumulated only a very tiny bit. If you do not dedicate the merit, you may have accumulated the same amount of merit, but it is quickly exhausted. Similarly, if you hold only one drop of water in your hand, it will fall or dry up. However, if you add that drop of water to the ocean, it becomes inexhaustible, even though it is still only a drop of water. For that reason, dedicating the merit at the conclusion of every practice session is very important.

STUDENT: I have problems with the second point. When I meditate, sometimes it is to help myself relax and feel less neurotic, and from that, I come back to connecting with my friends and other people. However, I feel that I do this for myself as well as others. Does the second point just include other people and not me? The attitude that I want to have is to include everybody—myself, as well as others.

RINPOCHE: This is a good question; you should clarify your doubts. I understand that you might hesitate to dedicate the merit if you think that by doing so you will lose the peacefulness and tranquility you have obtained. However, you never lose that. Think about the meaning of the phrase "for the benefit of all living beings." Since you are a living being, you are included. If I have a cake and I want to share it with everyone here, I also eat some myself!

The Importance
of Having a Spiritual Friend

In the mahayana tradition, a teacher who inspires us to virtue, and especially to cultivate and practice bodhicitta, is known as the spiritual friend. The term "spiritual friend" has a deeper meaning than it may seem at first glance. The Tibetan term, *geway shenyen* has come to be commonly translated as spiritual friend, but it literally means a virtuous friend or relative. Someone who teaches you how to be wholesome, virtuous, and not cause harm to yourself and others is very virtuous. The word friend or relative is used to suggest the closeness of the relationship. It is like a relative who is also your friend, and there is nothing closer than that.

As practitioners, we have a need for such a relationship. Though it is important to remember that you have the quality of enlightenment within you, the way to awaken that quality in practice is to have a spiritual friend who can assist you.

For example, if a particular language is not spoken in your country and no one you know speaks that language, it is completely unknown to you. However, although you have not learned that language, that does not mean you are incapable of doing so. You have simply not learned that language because you had no teacher to help you. If you do not speak Tibetan, it is not because you lack the intellect to do so, but because you have not had a teacher or a need to speak it. Now, if you happened to be in Tibet and were surrounded by Tibetans speaking their own language, you could potentially learn to speak Tibetan, even though it was previously unknown to you.

In the same way, as you begin the spiritual path, the subject of enlightenment is an unfamiliar one, and that is partly because you have had no spiritual friend. Because of your lack of training, combined with your confused state of mind, you have not experienced enlightenment up until now. However, that does not mean that you do not have the potential for enlightenment, in the same way that inexperience with a language does not mean that you do not have the potential to learn it.

If you do not speak Tibetan, you have not missed much. You have your own language, which is quite international. On the other hand, if you do not know the Dharma, you are missing a great deal. What you miss by not knowing the Dharma is the understanding of why all beings, rich or poor, young or old, experience suffering. As a result of not actualizing this quality of enlightenment, all beings go through unnecessary pain and suffering. The frustration, fear, and insecurity you yourself feel is the direct result of not having realized your own enlightened potential. It is necessary to liberate yourself from this suffering, and the only way to do so is to meet a spiritual friend. Without a spiritual friend, you have no way to familiarize yourself with the Dharma.

For someone to be an authentic spiritual friend, he or she must have a quality of realization and not simply have acquired a great deal of knowledge. Someone who has knowledge, but no quality of realization, is like a doctor who has no real experience in treating patients and, furthermore, no medicine. Such a person has intellectual knowledge, but is not experienced enough to help anyone. In the same way, a person who has learned about the Dharma intellectually, but has no personal experience, is not qualified to be a spiritual friend. A spiritual friend needs both knowledge and experience.

Even if someone is learned and experienced, these qualities are not sufficient to be a spiritual friend. If such person had not also developed compassion, it would be like a doctor who had closed his or her clinic out of a lack of compassion for those who are suffering. Therefore, the compassion required of a spiritual friend is the willingness to work tirelessly, without complaint or discrimination between rich or poor, young or old, male or female. This non-discriminatory attitude, combined with a readiness to work nonstop for others, is the definition of genuine compassion. This tireless effort might be compared to a farmer who cultivates grain and works very hard until harvest time. Such a farmer works full-time every day because he knows that if he takes a break, the grain will spoil. He is willing to work until the desired result is achieved. In the same way, the truly compassionate spiritual friend is willing to work tirelessly and without complaint. He does not discriminate against particular kinds of students, and he works with them until they show results. This friend serves as a source of knowledge, wisdom, and enlightened qualities. A virtuous friend with all of these qualities is really very rare.

We have accumulated a great deal of negative karma from our past lives, and this causes us to experience a continuous stream of suffering. The spiritual friend helps us to eliminate this stream of suffering. In the absence of this suffering, our obscurations can be purified and our enlightened qualities, which have been obscured by our confused state of mind, can be manifested. In this way, our virtuous friend becomes essential to the awakening of our own enlightened energy. Without the spiritual friend, experiencing our enlightened energy is not possible. Just as a flower cannot grow without soil, the spiritual friend is the ground for eliminating our neuroses and developing our enlightened qualities.

In addition to the qualities I have already mentioned—experience, learning, realization, and compassion—the virtuous friend must know the source of his own experience of enlightenment. Without knowing the source, this experience might be dangerous. In Tibet as elsewhere, there have been people who thought they had found a method to achieve enlightenment and then created new forms of practice based upon that method. However, what they developed was not sufficient because it was based on intellect rather than true realization and experience. They could fool many people into thinking they were presenting a true path, but there was no real ground or genuineness to their path.

This situation is similar to a person who is very intelligent and invents a language and claims it is the language of a specific country. He is able to make some people believe him but, when they visit that country, they find no similarity between the language he created and the one actually spoken there.

Buddhism in Tibet, China, and India takes its origin from the Buddha, the enlightened one. An authentic lineage that has come down to us unbroken from the Buddha is trustworthy, and it is safe to believe that the practices involved have a solid foundation. They have been proven over time. To understand who the spiritual friend is, it is very important to understand the origin of his or her lineage, the line of transmission. If there is no lineage, the path to enlightenment is vague. Every human being can trace his or her own lineage through parents, grandparents, and so forth. As authentic human beings, this is how you trace your history. In the same way, an authentic spiritual friend has to have a lineage. Nonetheless, we should not only consider the spiritual friend's lineage. In addition, the spiritual friend still must also have the qualities we have discussed: learning, realization, and true compassion.

As a student, you have responsibilities in relation to your spiritual friend. Once you find a spiritual friend, you must try to learn every experience and all the knowledge and wisdom that he or she has. Do not take that spiritual friend for granted, but try to understand what your spiritual friend is saying, and devote yourself to every detail of the practices you are given. Even though the practice may be difficult, try to understand the meaning and purpose of every aspect of it, and then apply it to yourself in order to attain realization. You will need tolerance to undergo the hardships of practice as you learn to apply the practices to your own life. A spiritual friend has realization and learning and is compassionate enough to teach you with tremendous patience.

In this world, there are people who are not authentic spiritual friends, but who speak beautifully and seem to be very intelligent. Therefore, you must make certain that the spiritual friend is authentic and not be fooled by beautiful words or flattery. You can tell the difference between the words of a spiritual friend and someone who has created a path without a lineage by thinking of this example: the nature of a fire, whether it is big or small, is to burn and give warmth. But a fire painted on a wall neither burns nor gives warmth, even though it looks the same as a real fire. This is true no matter how beautiful the painting is. The words of a spiritual friend contain warmth and have a certain weight, but words of flattery have no weight or warmth, even though they appear to be real. You can test the words of your spiritual friend by seeing if you feel a warmth that nourishes your heart and mind. That is how to determine if a spiritual friend is authentic.

Another point is that you cannot judge a spiritual friend by appearance. All virtuous friends will have the qualities I have described, but they come in many forms. They are not necessarily wealthy, since even a beggar could be a spiritual friend. They could be male or female, and attractive or not so attractive. What is important is not appearance, wealth, or gender, but the state of development of the spiritual friend.

As ordinary beings, it is difficult for us to understand who is realized within and who is not. Therefore the main question is: How can we determine who is an authentic spiritual teacher and who is not? How do we know who has realization and who does not? We must use logic to answer these questions because we do not have the realization to see the answers directly. With respect to this, at the beginning of your relationship with a spiritual friend, you have the right to examine the teacher before receiving teachings, empowerments, and so forth, in the same way that you have a right to examine gold before buying it. Pure gold remains pure, even if it is stored underground for years and even if it is cut into pieces.

You can examine the actions of the spiritual friend in the same way. As the days go by, does the spiritual friend's state of mind remain calm, and is his or her goal to benefit not only you but all sentient beings? If this teacher truly dedicates himself to leading all sentient beings to liberation, and you can see this over some period of time, you can regard that person as a spiritual friend.

The Buddha himself advised his students to examine teachers in this way, saying that sometimes you do not have to see something directly to know whether it is pure. The example he gave was fire: when we see smoke in the sky, we know there is fire in the valley and we do not have to see the fire directly. Similarly, when we see ducks flying, we know there is water nearby even if we do not see it. We can use our intellects to understand what we do not directly experience. In the same way, when we see an individual filled with unchanging love, compassion, and gentleness, we can be sure that person is an authentic spiritual friend.

Once you have determined that the spiritual friend is authentic, it is your responsibility to study and utilize his or her instructions diligently. At this point, do not be so concerned with finding the proper spiritual friend; be concerned with being a proper student by understanding and using the teachings that are given to you. If you hear teachings from the spiritual friend one day and forget them the next, you would not be making use of the spiritual friend's effort. That would be like using a tea strainer instead of a cup to get water: the moment the water is poured, it falls on the ground, and your thirst is not quenched.

It is important to uphold your responsibility in relationship to your spiritual friend. This means making use his or her advice and diligently practicing the teachings you have been given. You will not benefit simply by being in the presence of the spiritual friend; you have to make use of what you have been taught. This takes time. Your development will be gradual, and you should not expect overnight enlightenment. It is like pouring liquid from a full vase into an empty one; it takes time. In the same way, unfolding our enlightened qualities requires a gradual, step-by-step development.

Once you find a real, true spiritual friend, never give up on that relationship. Do not think, "Well, I found one, but I'll find another soon." Don't take that chance, because a genuine spiritual friend is rare and precious.

The Authentic Master
and the Authentic Student

This chapter, like the last one, is about the teacher-student relationship. However, the relationship with the spiritual friend that was described in the last chapter is concerned with entering and walking the bodhisattva path in a general sense, whereas this section is concerned with a very profound, effective, and auspicious level of practice within the bodhisattva path—namely, the direct recognition of the nature of mind, which is called mahamudra.

If buddha nature pervades every sentient being equally, we may wonder why some people are enlightened and some unenlightened. This is not the case because buddha nature is different in different people—it is the same in all beings. Rather, it is our own failure to recognize this nature and purify our obscurations that creates the different levels among us, making us advanced or ordinary, enlightened or unenlightened.

Ordinary people who have faith in such things may talk about the supernatural quality of enlightenment and the inconceivable wisdom of realized beings. As long as enlightenment seems exotic, we think we must search for it outside ourselves in some faraway place. However, regardless of how long we search, we will not experience enlightened qualities by looking outside of ourselves. These qualities are right here within us, and they have been inseparable from us since beginningless time. Realized people have not found enlightenment from another planet or deep within the Earth; they have followed the spiritual path here on Earth and practiced diligently in their daily life. In that way, they reached the fruition of their own potential and achieved inexhaustible happiness.

As ordinary beings, our biggest problem is that although we desire happiness, we do not know the correct method to obtain it, and so we search in the wrong places. We think that material goods or technological development will bring us contentment, and because we always depend on external things, we never find happiness. Finding changeless well-being is not a matter of getting external things; it is a matter of recognizing the essential nature of our minds.

At this point, we need to talk about what ignorance means at the deepest level. It is not particularly comfortable calling others ignorant, and we do not like to think that we ourselves are ignorant. However, in this context ignorance means not knowing that buddha nature is within us all of us. Because we do not recognize this enlightened potential, we seek enlightenment from an external person or object.

It is as though you held a precious jewel in your palm, but feel compelled to search for it elsewhere. It is not that you do not know how to look, or that the precious jewel does not exist. You do not see it because it is just too close to you, and so you search externally in every direction except right in front of you. Suddenly a very learned person comes along and says, "Look, the precious jewel is in your hand," and finally, you recognize it. This is what the Kagyu tradition calls "Buddha in the palm of your hand." There is no external being who can give us the enlightened quality or potential that we already have. Our enlightened potential is right here, and recognizing this is simply a matter of purifying ourselves.

Although it should be completely clear from this discussion that buddha nature is already within us, it is still necessary to be introduced to it by an authentic teacher. Such an introduction makes it possible for us to actually recognize the nature of our own minds. Ideally, an authentic teacher is a qualified master within a lineage, because we can be sure that a true lineage holder has all the skills and genuine qualities to transmit the teachings and introduce us to our own potential. An important characteristic of any spiritual master is that he or she has practiced and achieved some realization of the essential meaning behind the words of the teaching. In *The Rain of Wisdom*, Jamgön Kongtrül Lodrö Thaye explains that a spiritual master should be like a guide who has been there himself or herself. Such teachers have the power and the authority to point out the nature of mind.

If a teacher has only a conceptual understanding of buddha nature and does not know the essential meaning, he or she does not have the right to introduce the teaching to someone else. Not only that, that teaching would not be of much benefit to anyone. It would be as if I tried to teach English. I speak English by learning one or two words and memorizing them, scarcely knowing what they mean. I just repeat the words and do not know their full meaning, and I may even mispronounce them. Let's suppose I keep on repeating what I have learned, and then try to teach it to someone else. The person who learns English from me will not only miss out on the correct meaning, but will get the pronunciation wrong as well. There is the same likelihood for misunderstanding if someone tries to introduce the nature of mind simply through conceptual understanding. You need an experienced master to properly introduce you to your buddha nature.

Once we have been introduced to the buddha nature, a qualified teacher is also necessary to bring us to the fruition of full enlightenment. As I have explained, such a person has realization experience, and can therefore guide others on the path.

If an inauthentic teacher, someone with no experience of realization, tried to guide a student on the path through his own literal understanding, it would be like what happened to me during my visit to China some years ago. When I was in Beijing, I was supposed to visit a famous Buddhist monastery. Since I did not know where it was, I set out walking, and as I went along, I asked various people to give me directions. Now, most of the people I met did not know where the monastery was either. Because all human beings suffer from pride, they could not admit that they did not know the way. Instead, they pointed first in one direction and then in another, saying, "It is there." I followed the directions I was given, but each time I asked another person, that person sent me in a completely different direction. This went on all day, with many people pointing me in different directions, and I continued walking up and down, east and west, back and forth.

Luckily, I finally met an elderly lady who really knew her way around. She made me sit down, and she drew a diagram on a piece of paper showing me the correct route. With her guidance, I finally reached the monastery. That elderly lady was like an authentic teacher. She had experience because she had been there herself. Once you are lucky enough to meet such a person, if you follow his or her guidance, then every step you take will lead you closer to enlightenment. That is what is so inspiring about having an experienced spiritual master.

However, sometimes we may get too excited when we find an authentic teacher and encounter the limitless qualities of enlightenment. Suddenly, we lose all patience with the path because, having seen the result of enlightenment, we want to attain it immediately. This is the case for many of us who get inspired with the whole idea of enlightenment; we try so hard that we expect to succeed very quickly. When that doesn't happen and there is no enlightenment right away, we are disappointed. Therefore, we need to bear in mind that even if we have an authentic master, we must not expect instant enlightenment.

Enlightenment is like cultivating a seed. Once we have planted it in the ground, we have to be patient and wait. If we become excited thinking about what color the flower will be and what scent it will have, in our excitement we might dig up the soil we have just cultivated and try to pull up the plant, hoping to make it grow sooner. However, instead of producing a flower, we hinder its growth. Likewise, once we find an authentic master, we must be patient, tolerant, and careful not to jeopardize our spiritual journey. To become an authentic student requires that you practice with real diligence, with trust and confidence in the master, and without a great deal of expectation. If we are able to do that, and if our path is directed by the right person, then each moment of practice will bring us closer to enlightenment. We must practice patiently, without hope or doubt. By virtue of having a good teacher *and* of being a good student, you can reach enlightenment in one lifetime.

There is a proverb in Tibet that describes the qualifications of a good student. He or she must be like a mute, someone who does not speak, and at the same time he or she must be very persistent. The sense of the proverb is that the good student is mute because he or she has no doubts about the master or the teaching. Rather than speculating, the student simply works persistently to actualize the goal. We need to be like that. We need to work on actualizing enlightenment without too many questions, doubts, or expectations. We need to find an authentic teacher and be authentic students. That is what is necessary.

Cultivating a seed requires preliminary work. We cannot simply throw the seed onto hard ground; we must first turn over the earth to soften it. Similarly, if we want to apply more advanced teachings, we cannot avoid shamata meditation. Practicing shamata is like tilling the ground to plant the seed, and it is just as essential. Furthermore, we must not think that a set amount of shamata meditation is sufficient. Shamata has to result in a real sense of calm abiding before we can benefit from advanced practice. Without the consistent ability to rest with a peaceful mind, an hour or a month or even a year of shamata practice will not mean anything.

Let us say that we have prepared the soil where we want to plant a flower. The earth may be softened, but if we simply throw a seed onto it, a plant will not grow because the ground is too dry. We have to water the earth, and after we plant the seed, we have to continue to water it regularly. Similarly, it is not sufficient to just develop a sense of calm abiding through shamata. You have to cultivate loving-kindness and compassion for the welfare of all sentient beings at all times. Just as the plant requires constant moisture, the seed of enlightenment requires constant loving-kindness and compassion. These two qualities are essential because they enrich our ability to recognize the nature of mind.

Warmth is the third quality required to make a flower grow. In the fruition of enlightenment, warmth stands for wisdom, and it is as necessary to develop wisdom as it is to practice shamata and cultivate loving-kindness and bodhicitta. Just as soil, water, and warmth are required to grow a flower, so the three circumstances of calm abiding, loving-kindness and compassion, and wisdom must be present in order to reach the fruition of realizing the buddha nature.

We can talk about two kinds of wisdom in this context. Natural wisdom means that someone has the capacity to immediately understand both the literal meaning and the essential meaning of what is taught. Trusting wisdom, on the other hand, means that although a person may not have the sharpness to understand the essential meaning of the teachings, by trusting in the teacher and following the teacher's instructions, then that person will also achieve the fruition of enlightenment.

Natural wisdom is like having good eyesight. If somebody points in the direction of your goal, then you can see where to go. You do not need a guide. However, if you are blind, then you must depend upon someone who can see. If you let them guide you, then you will get to your destination. That is how it is with trusting wisdom: although your wisdom may not be particularly sharp at first, trusting the teacher will lead you to fruition.

Sometimes we may wonder why some students make great progress while we are left behind. Perhaps we think, "Maybe the teacher is not teaching me right, maybe he is discriminating. He gives better teachings to other people than he does to me." However, it is not a question of whether the teacher gives better or worse teachings or blessings. It is that we ourselves have not met the three required conditions: calm abiding, loving-kindness and compassion, and wisdom. Even if we are given profound teachings, if we do not try to understand and digest them, we will be unable to develop any fruition because we have not integrated the teachings and developed accordingly.

However, once we have met the first three conditions, if we progress with diligence we can quickly experience our goal. To do this, we need to accumulate merit. This means that we exert ourselves, maintaining good physical, verbal, and mental conduct. Such accumulation of merit will speed our growth and enable us to reach enlightenment much faster. At this point we will have met all the necessary conditions, and if we have an authentic master, then our prospects for enlightenment are no longer distant, but are in fact quite close.

We must understand, however, that the basic responsibility belongs to the student. It is your individual responsibility to apply the instructions of the authentic master. Even with a qualified teacher, we are still required to accumulate merit and practice diligently. Thus, to progress properly along the path, each practitioner must try to be an authentic student.

I would like to conclude with a short discussion on the topic of mahamudra. There are many excellent books on this subject, and since this book is an introduction to the Buddhist teachings, I will merely introduce you to it briefly. Most fundamentally, mahamudra is another name for the buddha nature that has existed within all beings from beginningless time. It is the wisdom or inherent enlightenment that exists in each one of us without exception, regardless of our nationality, race, or gender. Then, mahamudra practice is the path by which we prepare for and accomplish the recognition of this wisdom nature. The final outcome or fruition of mahamudra is the accomplishment of full and perfect spiritual enlightenment. In the Kagyu lineage, we regard the mahamudra teachings and practices as the very core or essence of our tradition. You need an authentic teacher to introduce you to mahamudra. If you find such a teacher, you are very fortunate indeed.

The Four Foundations of Mindfulness

The four foundations of mindfulness play an extremely important role in the Buddhist spiritual path. In fact, in terms of our inner engagement with this journey of practice, they are regarded as the beginning of training in wisdom. There are four basic contemplations which we can use to develop the quality of mindfulness we need, a mindfulness that provides a suitable grounding for the progression toward awakening that we are fully capable of making. These contemplations involve examining the body, the feelings, the mind, and outer phenomena.

We will approach these contemplations from the points of view of the three vehicles of Buddhism—the hinayana, mahayana, and vajrayana. It is important to note that although each vehicle has its own means of presenting the teachings and its own approaches to practice, the basis of the teachings is ultimately the same.

THE CONTEMPLATION OF THE BODY

The first contemplation is the contemplation of the body, and we will begin with the hinayana approach. Although our physical body is obviously impermanent, ordinarily we do not accept this fact. Not only is the body subject to death, it gradually deteriorates during our lifetime. Therefore, we concentrate on the physical body to learn about and understand its changes, as well as its final impermanence.

Usually when we think about the body, we consider it to be one solid entity. However, careful examination shows that this is not the case. The body is made up of many parts: the upper and lower body, the head, hands, legs, joints, and so on. There are internal parts of the body such as the lungs, heart, and other organs, and we also have skin, flesh, blood, bones, and marrow.

We can also break our body down according to the traditional system of the elements. The parts of our body that are solid and hard correspond to the earth element; whatever is moist and wet corresponds to the water element; the heat of the body is connected with the fire element; respiration and movement of the body are connected to the air or wind element; and the spacious and open aspects of the body correspond to the space element. Examining the body in this way helps reverse the habitual viewpoint of taking it to be one entity, and leads us to see it in terms of its many components.

Another way of contemplating the body is to consider impermanence and change. From the moment we are born, our bodies change constantly. First, we are infants, then small children, then adolescents, and finally we become adults. More subtle forms of change occur in our bodies as well, changes that happen in an instant. One moment we are hungry. Then after eating, our hunger is gone. We experience physical pain, and within moments the pain disappears. Such reflections help us understand the body's impermanent, changeable nature.

We can also investigate the notion that our bodies are pure. Let's consider a human corpse that has been left uncovered in a charnel ground. After several days, the body begins to rot, and insects and worms start eating the flesh. The only thing that prevents our bodies from going through that process now is that we are still alive. Other than that, our bodies are not any different from a corpse rotting in a cemetery. Such analysis helps overcome the fixation of thinking the body is inherently pure.

These various ways of analyzing our body also help us overcome our attachment to it, and inspire us to practice the Dharma. By recognizing the truth of our situation, we are motivated to apply the Buddhadharma in our lives while we have the opportunity and physical strength to practice. This physical body is, for the time being, connected with the mind. If we do not put it to good use and practice Dharma now, the body will eventually deteriorate without any benefit coming out of this life.

The following example helps illustrate this point. If you bought a pair of shoes, you would normally wear them to protect your feet and allow you to walk where you want to go. However, if you started walking without putting on the shoes and instead carried them over your shoulder, your feet would get sore. You wouldn't have made use of your shoes. Likewise, we can use our present body to practice the Dharma. Realizing that this body is subject to deterioration and impermanence, and realizing that what we thought of as pure is not pure, we will be strongly inspired to practice. This understanding helps us cut through our attachment to the body, and even learn to tolerate the physical pain and difficulties connected with practice.

Shantideva explains this situation by using the metaphor of the body as the servant of the mind. Since the mind is really the leader, it must learn how to guide the body, which is its servant. Otherwise, it is like hiring a servant and letting the servant sleep in your home while you do all the work yourself—it's impractical.

Detachment from our body does not mean that we do not take care of ourselves. We must learn to take care of the body by eating proper food and wearing clothing, just as a servant needs to be paid. However, when you pay a servant well, you then expect him or her to work. Relating this to our own situation, the job of the body is to practice Dharma. By practicing Dharma and not clinging to the body, the mind accumulates merit and develops spiritual realization. In that way, the mind profits from the physical effort of doing lots of practice, just as you profit when your employee works hard.

However, if we constantly pamper the body, which is like letting a servant relax without doing his work, the body does not gain any contentment. The more comforts we give it, the more it wants luxury and pleasure. Despite our attachment to the body, it is ultimately impossible to protect it from discomfort. In trying to obtain physical luxuries and comfort, we accumulate a great deal of negative karma connected with the mental afflictions.

Since it is not the body but the mind that accumulates negative karma when we seek physical comfort, the mind will continue to carry that negative impression at the time of death, when the mind and body separate. Knowing this, we contemplate the impermanence of the body in order to help remove attachment. This realization impels us to try to use the body in a way that is meaningful to the mind, by practicing Dharma and tolerating the physical difficulties and problems that come up in practice.

The mahayana or higher vehicle approach to contemplating the body is initially very similar to the hinayana. In the mahayana, we also try to recognize that the body is not a unified entity, but is rather composed of many parts. The mahayana approach takes things further than the hinayana by saying that even the names of the parts, such as the head, hands, legs, and so forth, are simply labels we have applied, and there is no reality to these designations either. Whatever we have labeled as a particular part can be broken down all the way to the smallest particles, atoms and beyond. In breaking down all the parts of the body, we do not arrive at any particular entity that can be pinpointed as real, true, or concrete. This establishes the unreal, insubstantial nature of the physical body. When we recognize this, we realize that the body that we are so attached to, the body that we take as real, does not really exist at all, in terms of our ordinary conception of existence. With that recognition, we can then rest the mind in that state of understanding.

This acknowledgment can establish the ground for the recognition of emptiness. When I talk about recognizing emptiness, I do not mean that this physical body suddenly disappears. Instead, meditating on emptiness refers to just what we have been talking about: when we carefully examine every part of the body from head to toe, we see that there is no real entity that exists on its own. Everything appears because of interdependence.

When we recognize the emptiness of the physical body, we experience a greater depth of loving-kindness and compassion towards all living beings because we understand that sentient beings constantly experience difficulties because they do not recognize the truth of emptiness. Realizing that the suffering of beings is based on this confusion, we will have a deeper experience of love and compassion.

The extraordinary perspective of the vajrayana teachings is very similar to the mahayana approach of breaking everything down and establishing that the body is empty. In vajrayana, having established the recognition of emptiness, the practitioner tries to realize through visualization and meditation that his or her own body is nothing other than the body of a deity. This deity's body is not solid or concrete, but it is similar to a rainbow or seeing one's reflection in a mirror: it is visible, but there is no solidity. This is the outstanding and extraordinary feature of vajrayana practice.

QUESTIONS AND ANSWERS

STUDENT: Do you recommend a regular practice of meditating on the impermanence of the body?

RINPOCHE: Not every day perhaps, but you have to do it quite often to overcome the viewpoint that the body is a permanent entity, and also to remove attachment to the body. To develop such understanding, we need to contemplate the subject often in order to implant the idea and not just understand it intellectually. However, this should not be taken as your only practice.

STUDENT: I work in a hospital and I see impermanence before my eyes all the time. For that matter, I can look in a mirror and see impermanence! Despite that, and no matter what has happened physically to me and my relatives, deep down inside I still don't believe in impermanence. I wonder if you could teach me how to light a fire under myself to know that this is all impermanent.

RINPOCHE: You have seen many examples of impermanence, but you have never contemplated or meditated on impermanence.

This is what prevents you from believing it deeply. Just seeing impermanence is not sufficient.

STUDENT: How does one go about meditating on impermanence? Would I meditate on seeing my body break down to a corpse or skeleton? Or does it mean contemplating that I will die like the people I see in the hospital?

RINPOCHE: The following meditation might be helpful. In order to do this practice, you need to completely believe that it is occurring. You should not think that you are simply meditating or pretending, but instead feel the reality of the situation. Let's say you wake up at 5:00 a.m., realizing that at 10:00 a.m. you will die. You have only five hours to live, and you truly believe this. So you set your alarm to go off at 10 a.m. You look at your watch, and as the time goes by you realize that you are getting closer and closer to death. As much as you try to prolong your life, time keeps moving forward. Throughout this period, you become more worried: "I should have done something that would have benefited me at the time of my death." This contemplation is helpful in recognizing impermanence and developing the idea of meditation or practice.

What determines whether this meditation is helpful or not is how serious you are about thinking that you only have five hours to live. If you really believe your life is ending and that you are getting closer to death, you will become very frightened. You will wonder what you can do, but there's no help. You realize that only the Dharma can help you.

In our modern era, we have watches that help us tell time. We can see the clock moving ahead every moment, and we know we are another second closer to death. This is a fact. Without this measurement of time, we would not realize that our life span is deteriorating. From the time we started this teaching until now, we have used up more of our life. This is what we are both conscious and not conscious of, the fact that we are all getting closer to death. The reason we need to recognize impermanence is not so we can develop anxieties or phobias: if all we do is worry about getting closer to death, then this recognition is of no benefit, because all you've done is develop fear, which causes suffering on top of your other difficulties. Instead, you must use this fear in a productive way by practicing the Dharma now, which will be of benefit both at the time of death and afterwards.

A similar situation would be the need to arrive at a particular destination before dark. You know the road you must take is quite difficult, and you know you don't want it to turn dark before you reach your destination. You look at your watch and check the time, and you realize you have to leave now and not just sit around. Through your knowledge of impermanence, you make a decision to leave right away.

STUDENT: If there is not a permanent body and there is not a permanent self, then what is the source of this?

RINPOCHE: Well, I did not say that this is not the accumulation of many parts. What is being said is that there is nothing permanent existing on its own without depending on something else. Nothing exists independently. Also, what we usually consider to be permanent is not permanent; what we consider to be one entity is not one entity; and what we consider to be pure is not pure.

STUDENT: What is the connection between developing a familiarity with the impermanent nature of body and mind and developing an understanding of shunyata?

RINPOCHE: Recognizing the impermanence of body and mind opens the door to recognizing emptiness or shunyata. Understanding impermanence is connected with realizing that there is no one entity that is the body, because the body is the conglomeration of many parts. As you know, breaking something down into its component parts can go all the way down to the atomic level. After that, it is possible to analyze what makes up the atom itself, and finally you reach the idea of shunyata or emptiness. When things are analyzed in this way, it makes sense to people. Otherwise, if the notion of emptiness is presented without a proper introduction, it is difficult to comprehend. Simply saying that nothing exists is very difficult for people to understand.

STUDENT: If you really think about impermanence, you would not realize it directly because you are dwelling on a thought. I understand it is important to see that the body is only a temporary shelter, like a hotel room for the mind. If you are thinking of meditating and say, "I'm going to meditate on this," you are not really meditating because you are not resting the mind, right?

RINPOCHE: Yes, and your question is a very good one. However, to rest the mind in non-thought we have to prepare ourselves and learn how to do it. It is very important to see that it is not a matter of forcing or expecting the mind to rest in that way.

However, keep in mind that these contemplations actually make use of our conceptual and analytical mind in a very effective and useful way, and it is important to see the value of that.

The Contemplation of Feelings

THE FOUR FOUNDATIONS OF MINDFULNESS

The second contemplation is the contemplation of feelings. Traditionally it is explained that there are three types of feelings: pleasurable, painful, and neutral. Pleasurable and painful feelings are easy to recognize, but it is more difficult to be aware of neutral feelings.

Feelings are also subdivided into mental and physical experiences. The physical experience of feelings is simply the sensation of touch. Whenever we feel the touch of something or somebody, this is a physical feeling. This is quite easy to understand.

The mental aspect of feelings consists of the experiences of the five sense organs engaging with the five objects of the senses, as well as whatever consciousness we experience from the meeting of the sense organs and the objects. For example, consider the process of vision. The physical sense organ related to vision is the eye, and the object of that sense organ is form. (*"Form" here basically just means the things we see with our eyes. Ed.*) When the eye meets with a form, we are happy if the form pleases us, and unhappy if it displeases us. The third possibility is that we experience neither happiness nor sadness, which is a neutral feeling.

A similar situation applies to the ear. Whenever we hear a sound, our physical sense organ, the ear, meets with the sound. If the sound is appealing to the mind, we enjoy it. If the sound is displeasing, we want to reject it. There is also a third situation, which is neutral, where we neither like nor dislike the sound. These three sorts of feelings—pleasurable, painful, and neutral—arise with all our physical senses: seeing, hearing, smelling, tasting, and touch.

In all these experiences, such as the eye seeing a form or the ear hearing a sound, the final judgment takes place in the mental consciousness. It may seem that the moment we hear a sound, the ear consciousness itself somehow knows the pleasant or unpleasant quality of that sound. The reality, however, is that the five senses are simply openings to the mental consciousness, which judges what the five senses meet with. For example, when the eye consciousness meets with a form, the eye consciousness does not judge if the form is attractive or ugly. It is the mental consciousness that does the judging and, after having judged, becomes attached to or rejects the experience.

You might wonder what the problem is with simply experiencing the pleasure and pain of feelings. From the point of view of Buddhist psychology, the problem is that these experiences stir up the kleshas. For example, when we experience something pleasant, we become attached to it. We then become involved in the attachment, and we want to maintain the pleasure and get more of it. On the other hand, things that displease the mind lead us to develop aversion, anger, resentment, and so forth. By being involved with all these mental afflictions, we accumulate negative karma. Neutral feelings, where there is neither attachment nor aggression, are connected with ignorance. Thus each of these three types of feelings contributes to the mental afflictions, which cause the accumulation of negative karma and perpetuate the experience of samsara.

In the hinayana approach, a practitioner realizes this fact and tries to rest the mind free from attachment and aggression. In the bodhisattva path (the mahayana), there is quite a different approach. The practitioner uses the experiences of pleasure and pain to nurture spiritual development, without trying to rest the mind free of attachment or aversion. In the bodhisattva practice, when we experience something attractive to the mind, we take upon ourselves the negative karma that all sentient beings have accumulated through attachment and passion. When bodhisattvas experience happiness, they learn to dedicate that happiness to all sentient beings. At the same time, bodhisattvas take the causes of negative karma connected to happiness upon themselves. In the same way, when we experience anything unappealing to the mind, we take on all the negative karma that beings have accumulated through anger and aggression. This is known as "accepting the nonvirtue and letting go of the virtue," which is the bodhisattva's way of nurturing the spiritual path. This approach is the integration of mind training in general, and tonglen (sending and receiving) in particular, with the contemplation of feelings.

In short, in the lesser vehicle we recognize the importance of not being involved with the mental afflictions of attachment, anger, and ignorance, and we try to abandon the causes of the mental afflictions. In the mahayana approach, we do not try to avoid the causes of the mental afflictions, but work to bring those experiences onto the path by learning to practice sending and receiving. In this way, we develop the possibility of benefiting others.

The tantric or vajrayana approach builds on the mahayana approach. This approach looks directly into the mental afflictions of attachment, anger, and ignorance. When you look directly into any of the kleshas, you come to realize the inseparability of the perceiver—the one who is experiencing the emotion—and the emotion itself. Therefore, there is nothing to be rejected or avoided, and nothing to be obtained. Through this approach, one can realize the wisdom aspect of the mind.

These are the different ways of approaching the same subject according to the three vehicles. Although each vehicle has a different approach, without a proper foundation in the hinayana and mahayana, we cannot learn to effectively apply the tantric approach. The tantric vehicle sounds very appealing but, appealing as it is, we have to approach it in a gradual way, through the proper stages of development.

In teaching about this, I often give the following example: a colorful flower is very nice to see and smell and touch. At the beginning, though, there is no flower. There is just a tiny seed, and it is very difficult to believe that a tiny seed has the potential for such beauty. If we really want to experience its potential, we have to be patient. The seed must be planted in the proper place and with the proper conditions. Then one day we will see it blossom fully. Likewise, although the tantric path seems to be very appealing, we have to proceed in a gradual manner.

QUESTIONS AND ANSWERS

STUDENT: If you have a very strong feeling about something, and you don't involve judgments and concepts, is the feeling even stronger because the mind is not involved? Is this the level of spontaneity we work on through meditation, leaving the mind out of it and just feeling?

RINPOCHE: Any sort of physical feeling could be experienced without the mental involvement of judging it as good or bad, but that is very difficult to do unless one is advanced in meditation. As a beginner, it is very difficult not to have concepts about our physical sensations, including pain.

With regard to mental feelings, as soon as you have a feeling, you automatically judge it as well. The gap between the judging and the feeling is so narrow that we cannot even detect it. Often we think that we have not made any judgment about our mental feelings, but that is just another form of distracted mind. Since your mind was so distracted by the feeling you experienced, you are not even conscious that you judged the feeling. This really shows the power of the distracted mind. In the vajrayana practice, the moment we recognize that we are having a feeling, we look directly into its essence—this is how we do the practice at an advanced level.

STUDENT: You mentioned the neutral feelings and said these were associated with ignorance. Could you explain that a bit more?

RINPOCHE: A neutral feeling is one where there is no clinging to the feeling as positive or negative, and thus there is neither attachment to nor rejection of the experience. However, because of the absence of wisdom, such feelings are associated with ignorance. The wisdom that allows us to realize the ultimate nature of our experience is not present. Thus, in the absence of such wisdom, there is ignorance.

STUDENT: To continue with this question, are you still creating negative karma with neutral feelings?

RINPOCHE: Yes. If you look directly at the nature of the neutral state, it is neither positive nor negative, so you have not accumulated negative karma. Still, this neutral state has many disadvantages. Although neutrality did not lead you to accumulate negative karma at that moment, it led you to indulge in laziness. Based on the absence of prajna, which is the wisdom of knowing the natural state of all phenomena, the neutral state of mind is a hindrance towards your motivation to practice and your realization of the ultimate state. Thus, although you may not be accumulating negative karma at that moment, the neutral state is still a hindrance.

STUDENT: With regard to these positive, negative, and neutral responses, let's say there is a situation where someone is treating you badly. Does this mean you could react by being mean in return, or by praying for them and doing sending and receiving, or by just being neutral? Is it correct to say that there are basically three choices? Should our goal be to practice on the mahayana level and never just be complacent?

RINPOCHE: Being tolerant when somebody is not treating you well, as well as doing the sending and receiving practice under those circumstances, depends on the genuineness and sincerity of your sending and receiving. At the moment when someone is causing you problems, if you are really able to do the practice, if you are free of anger and able to concentrate on sending and receiving, that is excellent. It is the best of all techniques.

However, if you are doing the sending and receiving practice, but inside you are burning with anger and hatred, then you are still cultivating negative karma. In that situation, simply telling yourself that you have done sending and receiving may not have helped eliminate the cultivation of negative karma. Thus, it all depends on how sincere you are.

There is a Tibetan proverb that goes, "Verbally you are claiming to be doing sending and receiving, but mentally you have the deepest hate and anger." If you are unable to do the sending and receiving purely, the second best approach would be to remain in the neutral state, without getting angry or trying to do sending and receiving.

STUDENT: I got a little confused when you said that if you are burning with hate do not do the sending and receiving practice, but go back to a neutral state. That confused me, because I thought in the neutral state, you did not feel positive or negative. Did you mean to go back to tolerance, and that tolerance is a neutral state?

RINPOCHE: No, the neutral state means not getting angry at all. You try not to pay attention to what is making you angry, and you do not let it affect your mind. Once you are angry, there is no neutral state. In the bodhisattva tradition, at the very moment you recognize that you feel angry, you think that you will take upon yourself all the negative karma that sentient beings have accumulated, along with the pain and suffering that result from this karma. By previously having this thought in practice, and by developing a mindfulness that knows anger to be a negative emotion that is destructive for self and others, a bodhisattva has the ability to practice sending and receiving. When it comes to being neutral, you try not to associate with the cause of anger at all.

The Contemplation of the Mind

THE FOUR FOUNDATIONS OF MINDFULNESS

Next, we will look at the contemplation of the mind. We often equate the idea of mind to the ego or self. Without examining the question carefully, we maintain a strong feeling that the self exists. In this contemplation, however, we look at the issue carefully: Is there really such a thing as the self?

The contemplation of mind builds on the understanding gained from the first contemplation, where we recognized that the body is nothing but a conglomeration of the five elements. Next, we need to ask, are the body and mind the same thing? Through careful analysis you can arrive at the conclusion that body and mind are not the same thing. After that, we need to start asking, "Where is the self?" Is it in the body? Is it the mind? If you examine all the parts of your body, you will not find a truly existing entity that is the self. Finally, you examine the mind. This is essentially what we are doing in this contemplation of mind. The outcome of this, as we will see, is that we will be unable to find an entity that we can actually pinpoint as the mind.

At that point, it becomes very easy to understand intellectually that there is no self. However, that is only at the level of intellectual thought. Deep down within ourselves we have the habitual pattern of ego-clinging, which has been ingrained and reinforced from beginningless time until now. Uprooting that pattern is very difficult because the foundation of this pattern is habitual attachment or fixation. Because of that deep level of habit, all situations of ego-clinging, whether they are attachment to the body or other fixations, are easy to understand—but difficult to uproot.

It is similar to wearing a particular shirt for a very long time and never washing it. After many months, the shirt would be really dirty, with all sorts of stains. At that point, we might think that the stains are an integral part of the shirt because they have appeared together for so long. But they are not. The shirt can be cleaned, although it may need repeated washing to get all the stains out. This is similar to the process of meditation after we have understood intellectually that the physical body is impermanent and that there is no self. We have to meditate on this repeatedly in order to uproot our habitual pattern of believing that a self exists. Through meditating that there is no self, you will one day develop a new pattern; we are reversing a confused habit, and there will come a time when the meditation becomes deeply ingrained. Therefore, the initial steps of understanding impermanence, detaching from the body, and realizing that there is no solid self will help uproot confusion if these steps are applied in conjunction with meditation practice.

When we meditate in this manner, we are resting the mind in the true reality. In the past, we were accustomed to being involved in the illusions and fabrications of the mind, so it was quite difficult to recognize the true nature of body and mind. The result of genuine meditation is that you become detached from clinging to your body, uproot the idea of a self or ego, and, as a result, you also uproot your mental afflictions.

However, people who are new to meditation sometimes expect that the moment they meditate, there will be auras around them, or that other unusual spiritual things will happen. That is a serious misinterpretation of what meditation is really about. Meditation simply means knowing and being in a natural state. Here "natural" means freedom from the mental afflictions. That is the true realization of meditation.

Along with that, the genuine outcome of being learned in the philosophical view of Buddhism is to be naturally gentle and kind in all your behavior. This comes about because all Buddhist teachings emphasize avoiding harming others. Having understood the negative quality of such harmfulness, we would naturally abstain from any physical action or speech that might hurt others. That is the true understanding of Buddhism.

THE DIFFERENT TYPES OF CONSCIOUSNESS

The psychological teachings of Buddhism break the mind down into different kinds of consciousness, which offers an in-depth way of contemplating the mind. According to the hinayana approach to those teachings, the mind is divided into six kinds of consciousness. For example, the eye consciousness, which has the capacity to see form, is not the same as the ear consciousness, which has the capacity to hear sounds. Each of these sense organs can experience a different consciousness: form, sound, smell, taste, and physical touch. These five are known as physical sense consciousnesses.

The sixth is the mental consciousness, which is the one that conceptualizes and judges. It evaluates and discriminates among the perceptions arising from the physical senses, and it is also capable of reflecting on the past and planning for the future. Past and future events are not connected with the physical senses, which are only experienced in the present. These are the six aspects of the mind according to the lesser vehicle.

In the mahayana teachings, there are two more types of consciousness added to these six. The first is called the klesha consciousness. The klesha consciousness is the fixation upon self or ego. It is the strong fixation that "I exist," and that the "I" is real. This fixation is the way our ignorance operates, so to speak, and as we've said, it is a deeply ingrained habitual pattern.

Going along with the basic ignorance of ego fixation, the klesha consciousness can be subdivided into other kleshas that arise, all based on our fixation. The subdivisions are attachment, anger, arrogance, doubt, and wrong belief. The klesha consciousness really consists of the operation of these different functions of these kleshas.

They are slightly different from each other in their characteristics, but if you think about it, they all center on our ego fixation.

The klesha consciousness of wrong belief requires some explanation. Fundamentally, we can say that whenever you have a fixed idea, that is your belief. Fixating on that idea or belief as real and true, and not having the willingness to be open to other ideas or change your point of view, is known as the klesha consciousness of wrong belief.

Although our minds are, in their ultimate nature, pure, we do not have the mental strength to maintain this state. Therefore, we are under the influence of the kleshas. Being under the influence of the different types of kleshas leads us to accumulate karma, which is the basis of all six realms of samsara. An analogy for how we have lost control is to say that the nature of our minds is like a good king who has fallen under the influence of deceptive ministers. Although the king himself wants to do what is right, he is led into incorrect actions because of the ministers' skillful deception, and is not aware that he is doing wrong. When we are under the control of the different aspects of the klesha consciousness and are not able to recognize the natural state of mind, it is the same situation.

However, we must not look only at the negative aspects of the mind. There are positive qualities as well. A positive aspect of mind is analogous to having a healthy, decent minister influence the king toward proper understanding and action. Such a healthy, positive state gives the mind the capacity for tremendous confidence. Having learned about the value of Dharma practice, the mind also has the capacity of diligence, the diligence to practice consistently and overcome laziness. Once we have recognized that the negative qualities of body, speech, and mind are in fact negative, our minds have the capacity to develop mindfulness, and to cease indulging in such actions.

In addition, through being diligent in the practice of not engaging in negative actions of body, speech, and mind, and by the power of mindfulness, our minds have the capacity to experience wisdom (prajna). Based upon the experience of prajna, the mind can eventually come to know the truth of all phenomena. With this knowledge, the mind can then rest in a Samadhi, unmoved by the kleshas. The mind also has the capacity to develop loving-kindness and compassion, which are the key factors for benefiting all sentient beings. It is not a question of the mind lacking positive qualities— the mind has all manner of positive qualities—but we must make an effort to develop to the point that it is not controlled by the kleshas.

The eighth aspect of consciousness is known as the ground consciousness or alaya consciousness. It is the part of our mind where our habitual patterns associated with the kleshas are imprinted. The alaya consciousness itself is a neutral thing; it is neither good nor bad, neither positive nor negative. It is also important to understand that the alaya consciousness is not something substantial.

Since alaya consciousness is neutral, you can cultivate positive habitual patterns or negative habitual patterns. Under the right circumstances and conditions, whether arising in this lifetime or in future lifetimes, the ground consciousness brings about the fruition of the seeds that were imprinted. Therefore, the function of the ground consciousness is to take on the imprints of habitual patterns, and also to give rise to the result of those patterns. Whether the klesha is attachment, aggression, or neutrality, a sort of imprint is made in the alaya consciousness. By associating with the kleshas you implant negative habitual patterns in the alaya consciousness; and as we know, the outcome of negative habitual patterns is suffering.

That is how the alaya consciousness works for ordinary confused beings, but it can also be understood to have two aspects. In its true reality, it is regarded as a wisdom alaya, which is another term for the inherent buddha nature. Thus, there is the alaya of confused consciousness, and also the alaya of wisdom awareness. The wisdom alaya is what is experienced by an awakened being. In the absence of the kleshas, all the enlightened qualities of the buddha nature are fully realized.

REMEDIES

Through our mindfulness of mind, we become aware of its positive and negative aspects. We do not need to be overwhelmed by the negative aspects because there are remedies that help transform the mind. In the hinayana tradition, we transform the negative aspects of mind by practicing shamata, sitting meditation. On this path, we would avoid any behavior that is unwholesome, improper, or negative. Instead, we adopt a wholesome, positive conduct and attitude.

In the mahayana or bodhisattva approach, we do not particularly need to avoid what seems to be negative or adopt what seems to be positive. Instead, we try to rest the mind in the meditative state known as the natural state of all phenomena. By resting the mind in this natural state, we develop the prajna that cuts through the ignorance of viewing our experiences as concrete.

Furthermore, the main practice of the bodhisattva is not just resting in this natural state, but also developing loving-kindness by understanding the suffering of all sentient beings. Loving-kindness, again, is the wish to provide happiness to each and every sentient being, without discriminating between friends and foes. Bodhisattvas have the wish to provide beings with happiness, and are joyful whenever sentient beings actually do experience happiness. There is natural, spontaneous joy in the aspiration to establish all sentient beings in the state of lasting happiness. On the bodhisattva path, we uproot and eliminate jealousy not by adopting or rejecting anything, but by learning to love all sentient beings equally.

Likewise, practicing and perfecting compassion in the bodhisattva path naturally uproots anger. When we are angry, there is aggression, as well as an intention to hurt or cause pain to another. But whenever we are compassionate, our intention is to alleviate and remove suffering. These two states of mind are totally contradictory, so when you have established the compassionate mind, you naturally cancel out the mental affliction of anger.

The same is true with regard to the elimination of greed. Why are we greedy? Often it is because we are frightened of experiencing poverty and loss, and we do not recognize the importance of others and the importance of benefiting them. Based on this sense of self-absorbtion and the fear of losing our own well-being, we are unable to be generous. In learning to practice the bodhisattva path, we focus on the importance of others, wanting to benefit all living beings and therefore lessening our own importance. In that way, the mahayana practitioner becomes detached from selfish happiness. As practitioners, we become willing to go through any extent of hardship to provide happiness for others, and this eliminates the mental affliction of greed.

The bodhisattva path also helps us cut through ego-clinging, which is regarding ourselves as being most important. Due to selfishness, self-importance, and preoccupation with our own personal needs, we have failed to realize the needs of other sentient beings. Once we turn our mind toward understanding the needs of others, we become less attached to our self.

As well, the skillful means of the bodhisattva path allows us to dissolve the mental affliction of arrogance. In the past, we thought of ourselves as important, superior, and more intelligent, and we looked down on others as inferior. As a bodhisattva, we regard others as more important. We also take an attitude like a mother looking after her child. A mother does not think of the child as stupid or ignorant, and she is willing to go through any degree of hardship to provide for her child's needs. In the same way, being willing to go through hardships to benefit sentient beings eliminates arrogance.

The bodhisattva path also cuts through wrong views. In particular, there are the wrong views of eternalism or substantialism on the one hand, and nihilism on the other. Our instinctive substantialist view involves the fact that, as ordinary confused beings, we view all phenomena as being real, true, and concrete. To counteract this, we use a similar approach to the one used in the contemplation of the body, we use the analysis that breaks everything down into many parts and finds that nothing is permanent or independent, and this uproots our fixation on solidity. The wisdom of the bodhisattva outlook uproots nihilistic views as well, because we recognize the truth of karmic cause and effect. We see that virtuous actions allow our minds to experience qualities such as wisdom, diligence, compassion, and loving-kindness. We also see that through unvirtuous action, we will experience the suffering associated with the mental afflictions. In that way, we arrive at the understanding that virtuous activity leads to the experience of positive qualities of mind, and unvirtuous activity leads toward negative states of mind. Thus, by believing in karma and its result, we do not fall into the extremes of nihilism. Through the means of the bodhisattva path, the emphasis is not on uprooting the kleshas directly. Instead, by developing the good qualities of loving-kindness, compassion, prajna, and so on, negative qualities are naturally and effortlessly removed.

In the mahamudra approach to meditation, we come to understand that our distraction causes us to experience the emotional states associated with the kleshas and prevents us from recognizing the true nature of the mind. What we learn through applying the teachings is to not let our minds be distracted. Resting the mind in non-distraction, free from engagement in the mental afflictions, is what is known as resting the mind in the natural state.

To rest the mind in its natural state, we must diligently practice meditation. At the beginning, when we are not accustomed to this kind of resting, it is hard to maintain a state of non-distraction or stillness. As we apply the practice consistently, however, we can develop the possibility of resting the mind naturally, free from distraction. But unless we work to develop this through practice, theoretical understanding of such knowledge will not be sufficient to eliminate distraction. If someone were to understand this intellectually and wanted to experience the non-distracted state of mind, they might try to repress or reject thoughts. Repression of thoughts is not the way to achieve this; it is very different from that. The experience of meditation is the only way to see this. There is no way that it can be discussed conceptually because resting the mind is beyond words. You cannot say, "This is it," and you cannot say,

"This is not it." The natural state of resting the mind simply has to be experienced through one's own practice of meditation.

An individual who practices Dharma and meditation diligently can learn to rest the mind in its natural state, and this leads into the authentic vajrayana level of practice. We begin to realize that the mind is similar to a mirror, in the sense that what is reflected depends on where the mirror is facing. If a mirror is facing toward the ground, it has the capacity to reflect the earth and anything on it—garbage, muddy water, or anything. If the mirror is turned toward to the sky, it reflects the spaciousness of the blue sky or the clouds. But the mirror isn't inherently any of those reflections. If you learn not to be involved in the mind's distractions, if you learn to turn your mind away from the neurotic thoughts that cause all your emotional upheavals, your mind becomes free. Having turned away from that, you can experience all the enlightened qualities, and all the deities as well.

At this point, you also realize the wisdom that is beyond any conception. We usually think that samsara and nirvana are two different places, and so we separate them as totally different things. In fact, the experience of samsara and nirvana are within your mind, and your experience is based upon whether you turn your mind toward the distraction of experiencing the kleshas or towards the ultimate nature of mind, in which there is the experience of every kind of wisdom.

Thus we could say that we are presently ordinary sentient beings but, at the same time, we are enlightened beings as well. Which aspect we actually experience depends on the orientation of our minds.

QUESTIONS AND ANSWERS

STUDENT: Let's say you're in a situation where people make you angry, where you feel aggression coming up and you'd like to hurt them in some way. In order to act positively, what would be the skillful action in that situation? You mentioned that in the hinayana, you would try to get that sort of situation out of your life and protect yourself from it so the kleshas don't arise. You also mentioned the mahayana approach, where you would remain in the midst of all positive and negative experiences. But how can the mind act positively in a negative situation?

RINPOCHE: The reason there are the different approaches of hinayana and mahayana is that people have different psychological capacities. Beginners can relate to the hinayana aspect of dealing with the kleshas because it is obvious that the kleshas create problems for ourselves and others. Thus, the obvious approach for a beginner is to try to keep a distance from the causes of the kleshas, to try to avoid the things that incite us to anger, attachment, and so forth.

Let's look at the mahayana level of practice. The prefix "maha" means greater. This means that a practitioner of this path has developed some greater degree of psychological strength or capacity, that the kleshas cannot disturb his or her one-pointed concentration. When you have developed that quality, then you are within the category of the greater vehicle. At this level, when you encounter an object that could cause you to become angry, the emotion is not powerful enough to force you into getting angry because of your mental stability. Instead, at the moment someone creates a potentially difficult situation either verbally or physically, you manifest compassion. That is the outcome of mahayana practice, because you have already developed strong compassion.

You develop compassion for someone who is creating a nuisance by coming to understand that this individual is creating these problems because they are strongly attached to their own well-being. Being unaware of the needs of others, this person is trying to gain something for themselves, and so they create problems. Understanding that, you would have greater compassion for them. In addition, as a mahayana practitioner you also realize that the person is accumulating lots of negative karma through their actions. This creates another reason for you to act with compassion.

If a person becomes angry with you and expresses it either physically or verbally and you react by returning that anger, at that moment, you are not a practitioner because you are creating negative karma and enabling the other person to create negative karma as well. Such behavior is not the answer. Instead, you try to have tolerance, and you know that when you are tolerant, you are accumulating great merit. At the same time, do not be attached to the merit, but dedicate it to the person who angers you because this person has accumulated negative karma. Think to yourself, "May this person's negative karma be purified by my patience and tolerance." This display of mental strength is mahayana practice.

STUDENT: I can understand that the answer is tolerance. But what if I'm tolerating something I don't necessarily like tolerating—in other words, if I feel compassion after an interaction is over, but at the moment it's occurring I don't feel compassionate at all. I know in situations like that I can understand the other person's actions intellectually, but if I don't feel total and complete compassion, I'm just tolerating them.

RINPOCHE: If you understand this outlook intellectually, then the rest has to come with practice. You build this strength of compassion by gradually becoming more familiar with this approach. It is a matter of training the mind.

STUDENT: You said that we have to develop and practice compassion towards all sentient beings. Now, I am a sentient being as well, so does that mean it's a two-way street and I have to practice some tolerance for myself?

RINPOCHE: In the past, we constantly maintained a self-centered attitude and tried to protect our own interests. As a result, we developed many mental afflictions—anger, jealousy, and so forth— and we accumulated negative karma. Therefore we are actually the ones who lost out, because we are the ones who will have to experience the outcome of that negative karma. Focusing on ourselves alone has never brought us any accomplishment.

What we need to do is really develop love and compassion for all sentient beings. When we do that, we accumulate merit—a positive karmic accumulation. The merit enables us to reach buddhahood. Therefore, ultimately, we ourselves will benefit from developing genuine love and compassion for others. With this understanding, you can see that the compassionate outlook toward all beings is beneficial both for others and yourself.

It is similar to the following example. Let's say you are working for the government or in some form of service. You work wholeheartedly with a generous attitude, and you dedicate a great deal of your time and effort. When you are acknowledged for all this valuable work, you receive a promotion, a good reputation—and probably, a good salary. By working hard for the organization, you obtained benefits for yourself. In the same way, developing compassion for others will bring benefits to you in the long run.

STUDENT: You mentioned shamata meditation as a hinayana practice. I had understood that the shamata practice goes all the way through the mahayana and the vajrayana, and I was just wondering if you would comment on that.

RINPOCHE: That is true. Shamata means developing the calm-abiding quality of the mind. Precise stability of mind is necessary in all levels, and that is why shamata practice is used in all the different vehicles: the hinayana, mahayana, and vajrayana. However, the way the calm-abiding mind is used in each vehicle is slightly different.

In the hinayana, when we develop stability, we try to use this stability to one-pointedly contemplate impermanence, to consider the change and deterioration of the body from infancy until death. It can also be used to contemplate the fact that all objects in the world are not one solid thing, but can be broken into many particles. In the mahayana tradition, calmness of mind is used to rest the mind in the ultimate nature of phenomena, free from concepts and dualistic mind. In the vajrayana, the stability of mind is used more in concentration on the deities and other practices. The mental qualities arising from shamata are necessary in all the vehicles, but are used differently in each.

The Contemplation
of Phenomena

The fourth contemplation is the contemplation of phenomena. As ordinary, unenlightened beings, the habitual way we relate to outer phenomena—that is, perceivable objects—is to habitually view them as real and separate from ourselves. We fixate on outer phenomena as concrete, permanent, and true. Along with that fixation, we also develop emotional patterns, such as attachment.

What is the process that brings about this fixation? When consciousness is involved with outer phenomena, various experiences and feelings arise. We think that when we perceive a particular object, it causes us to experience a particular feeling. Actually, all the feelings that arise when we experience outer phenomena are based on what we have cultivated in the alaya consciousness in the past—and by the past, we mean not just the past in this life, but our past lives as well. When experiences arise, the conditions are met that ripen the seeds already cultivated in the alaya, so the experience is actually the fruition of a past habit. The result has just been waiting to ripen, and the ripening takes place at a given time due to the meeting of proper conditions.

Because beings have cultivated different patterns in their alaya consciousness, they do not have the same reaction even if they perceive the same objects. As human beings, we have what is known as a common accumulation of karma. Due to this collective karma, we see everything around us in a similar way. This could also be called a common imprint of karmic patterns on each person's alaya consciousness. However, each individual will feel something different when seeing a particular object; we do not all have the same feelings in terms of pleasure, pain, and neutrality.

As well, the importance of a particular type of object may be completely different for different beings. For example, human beings can see plants and trees, and animals see these things as well. Certain animals live on plants and perceive them as part of their survival. As humans, we do not experience the importance of plants in that way. There are also animals that see plants, but cannot use the plants to survive because they eat animal flesh. Then, there are animals that live in bodies of water, and they will die if you take them out of the water. As human beings, we can also see water, but its purpose is different for us. In fact, water is potentially dangerous for humans. Therefore, although beings may see the same thing, the significance of any particular object differs.

Therefore, there is no ultimate reality to the objects that we perceive: a home for one being could be dangerous for another. This is very much related to the teaching that there are six realms with six types of beings based upon their accumulation of karma. In actuality, though, there are not six separate realms. It is the mental state of beings that divides our experience into these six realms. This very monastery where we are gathered today, this very shrine room, is the six realms. For example, as human beings, we have the collective karma to see this shrine room as a beautiful room with a polished wooden floor that we enjoy very much. For a hell being, this same floor would not be wood. It would be like a hot iron upon which they are being burned. Hungry ghosts would experience this room as hot and dry, like a burning, sandy desert where they would be hungry and thirsty. For a being from the god realm, this floor would be a paradise composed of precious jewels.

The fact that individuals within the six realms perceive the same place differently due to habitual patterns created by karma shows that there is no such thing as a real or actual object. Ultimately, our experienced reality is only the manifestation of karma. If we can understand that, then we will be able to disengage from our usual notion of reality, the notion that phenomena are objectively real.

I will try to explain the idea of the nonreality of phenomena with the following example. Two people are asleep; one is having a pleasant dream in which he is walking in a beautiful park, and the other person is having a nightmare and experiencing a great deal of pain. Now, if we ask what causes these two individuals to have these dreams, the answer would be that it is because each is asleep. And as long as they are asleep, their experiences seems real to them. One person is having an enjoyable experience, and the other is suffering, but the moment they wake up, they see that there was no reality to either of their experiences. If you tried to search for the good dream—the park he visited, and so on—you would find that no such thing exists. The park was a mentally induced image. The same is true with regard to the individual who was experiencing the negative dream. When this person wakes up, he will realize that all the causes of suffering had no reality; the experiences were simply a state of mind. That is what is meant by phenomena being beyond any perceived existence. Like dreams, all phenomena ultimately have no reality.

We experience these different states within our minds due to our habitual patterns. And because of our mental afflictions, we do not realize that our habitual patterns cause these experiences; instead, we perceive our experiences of phenomena as real, true, and permanent. Clinging to phenomena as real and true is where we lose our way. There is no reality, truth, or permanence to outer phenomena, but we do not recognize this because of our attachment.

All phenomena are also impermanent with regard to time. When you say something happened last year, this indicates that it has passed. You cannot create what happened last year now, which shows that a change has occurred. Even what happened yesterday is in the past, and cannot happen today. In terms of the seasons, we see a great difference between summer and winter. In the summer, the environment is very warm and green, and in the winter, it is very cold. Curiously, we may not recognize these changes as symbols of the general impermanence in our lives, but simply cling to the idea that the phenomena we perceive are real and solid. This fixation leads us to experience great pain and loss.

The impermanence of outer phenomena, such as last year, this year, summer, fall, winter, and spring may not be difficult to relate to because these are examples of the grosser aspects of change. However, subtle or moment-to-moment changes happen each instant. These momentary changes occur so quickly that we do not always perceive them. As a result, we think that things are permanent and do not recognize that they are impermanent.

For example, you may go to a particular river and say, "I see the river." A year later when you go to the same place, you say, "I see the river again." Actually, the river is not the same at all. Every second the water has been flowing, so it has changed. This is the way we label and fixate on things as being the same, when they are not.

Phenomena are deceptive. This is not because phenomena have an intention to deceive us. We are deceived because we do not recognize this rapid change, and as a result we fixate upon phenomena as being real, true, and permanent. But phenomena are not real, true, or permanent. Therefore, our beliefs about phenomena and the actual nature of phenomena do not coincide. This gives us pain, and we feel that we are deceived by outer phenomena. In fact, we have deceived ourselves.

Objects like our house, a room, or a table are things we think of as solid, as entities unto themselves which exist independently. In truth, they do not really exist independently. They are all an accumulation of many smaller parts. This is true even of a particle of sand. There is no such thing as something existing independently, even though we may perceive things that way.

Similarly, the perceiver changes. The person who saw something a year ago and the person who sees it now are different. We think the mind remains the same, but perceptions change from moment to moment. You can dwell upon what you perceived before, but even your experience of dwelling upon past perceptions will change. The one who is doing the dwelling is new, and it is not the same mind because the mind also changes every instant. And it's happening so fast! We do not recognize the speed of its movement, and so we cling to the concept of a permanent perceiver. And because we do not realize the impermanence of the perceiver and the impermanence of what is being perceived, we suffer when experiences end. We do not want things to end because we have attachment to things as real and permanent, but they do end because the nature of everything, including the mind, is change. Thus, both the perceiver and the phenomena being perceived are always in a state of flux.

We need to ask ourselves what the benefit is of recognizing impermanence, and what the disadvantage is of not recognizing impermanence. We'll start with the disadvantage. By not recognizing impermanence, we give birth to the klesha of attachment. Since everything is subject to deterioration, when that experience or phenomena ceases, you have a strong sense of loss. From that feeling of loss, you may develop a great deal of anger, frustration, and many other kleshas, which create karma within your alaya consciousness.

On the other hand, the advantage of recognizing impermanence is that even though you experience phenomena and then experience the cessation of those phenomena, you do not really become attached because you know things are impermanent and not real. If you are free from attachment, then no matter what happens, you do not create any karma. When phenomena cease, you do not feel loss because you knew that they would eventually end. In turn, no anger or frustration arises. As a result, you do not create karma, and because you do not create any new karma, you gradually experience liberation.

It is similar to building a fire. If you start a big fire and then stop adding wood to it, it will eventually burn down and extinguish itself. Otherwise, if you constantly add more wood, you will maintain the fire indefinitely. If you want to stop the fire, it makes no sense to add more wood to it. Likewise, when you stop cultivating habitual patterns, and therefore stop creating karma, liberation is possible.

Both the hinayana and mahayana traditions recognize samsara as being a trap where we are conditioned to experience pain and suffering. They both regard samsara as like a nest of poisonous insects to be avoided at all costs. With that sort of outlook regarding samsara, the path of the lesser vehicle is to become liberated by not having attachment to the poisonous nest. Without attachment, you will not be attracted to it. An animal that is trapped in a cage will always try to get out. Likewise, those on the hinayana path concentrate on becoming liberated from the trap of samsara by viewing it as poisonous and dangerous.

The mahayana or bodhisattva tradition realizes that phenomena have no reality, so beings on this path do not develop fear of samsara, and they do not have any sense of dislike towards any phenomena. If you see something as not real, you will not develop fear, dislike, or anger. At the same time, the bodhisattva recognizes that sentient beings, who still believe in the reality of phenomena, suffer tremendously due to their mental confusion. The bodhisattva then develops great compassion and loving-kindness, as well as great willingness to benefit sentient beings and lead them out of their confused state.

In the vajrayana, tantric practitioners are not only aware of the unreal nature of dualistic phenomena, but because of the great depth of their spiritual development and because of their accumulation of merit, they try to transform phenomena into a buddha field or a pure land. The transformation is an outcome of their own merit, which enables them to see any given phenomena as a buddha field, and experience it as such. In actuality, nothing external has changed.

Let's look, for example, at the pure land of Amitabha, which is called Dewachen. If your mind is pure and if you have enough accumulation of merit, wherever you are right now is Amitabha's realm. When the mind is not pure, when it is obscured, then wherever you are right now could be a hell realm. We are not speaking of two different realms when we refer to a buddha field or samsara. The difference between samsara and nirvana has to do with your state of mind, the degree to which it is free from negative karma. It is also a question of the strength of your merit.

The point is that the phenomena have not changed, but our perception of phenomena has changed. We remain in the same location, but our perception transforms it into a different realm. It's similar to wearing eyeglasses: if three people are given three different colored eyeglasses —green, red, and blue—and are told to look up into the sky, the one who wears red sees the sky as red, the one who wears green sees the sky as green, and the one who wears blue sees it as blue. The color of the sky is perceived to be different by these three people because the color of their glasses is different. Likewise, people perceive phenomena differently because their mental states differ. Therefore, the tantric practitioner, having deeper realization of practice as well as a greater accumulation of merit, is able to see the enlightened quality of phenomena.

Therefore, when we talk about learning to get rid of suffering and experiencing liberation, it is really very simple. We are not trying to get to another destination or another world. It means that we should avoid activities that are associated with negative karma, and adopt and practice activities that are associated with positive karma. We should create a habitual pattern of positive activities. By the virtue of that accumulation of merit and the absence of negative karma, we will experience this very place—this very life—as a pure realm. And that is happiness.

KARMA

There are two other points I would like to make that relate to the four foundations of mindfulness as well as practice in general. The first is about karma, which plays a very significant role in the lives of all sentient beings. The accumulation of habitual patterns from past lives—and this one— is our karma. There are people who enjoy health and long life, and then there are others who experience sickness or sudden death. That is due to their karma. Habitual patterns of the kleshas—attachment, anger, jealousy, pride, ignorance, and greed— are the cause of the six realms. These are the seeds that cause the six realms to exist. At the time of death, due to the strength and power of whatever klesha is predominant in your mind, you will experience the manifestation of the particular realm associated with it. Although that realm has no true existence, you will experience it due to the strength of your karma.

We are human beings now. When we die, however, there is no guarantee we will experience human birth again. Believing that we are guaranteed a human rebirth is just a form of self-deception. When an ordinary human being dies, rebirth in a particular realm will manifest due to the strength of that person's karma. Therefore, uprooting the six kleshas is essential in order to prevent us from experiencing birth in the six realms. We do this by learning to develop habitual patterns of positive actions, disengaging from mental afflictions, and pacifying strong negative emotions by applying Dharma practices. In that way, we uproot past habitual patterns because we do not strengthen them in the present and future.

We can learn from the example of a child who builds a sandcastle at the seashore. The moment the waves come in and wash the sandcastle away, the child cries because he or she put so much work into building it and believed it was something real. As an adult, you know it is just a sandcastle, so you not develop attachment, anger, or sadness when it is washed away. That is the kind of outlook you need to maintain with regard to phenomenal experiences. With such an attitude, you do not accumulate karma.

Therefore, once we learn that phenomena are not real, we will not become attached to them. We also will not try to reject phenomena, but instead we can learn to enjoy them.

MEDITATION IN DAILY LIFE

The other point I would like to make is about integrating practice into our daily lives. Often we think we are not doing enough for our own benefit, and this is quite true. You can make sure you are really doing enough to benefit yourself by consistently practicing the Dharma. This does not mean you have to abandon your family, home, or career. You need your livelihood, and it would not necessarily make sense to abandon all these things. What it *does* mean is you need to make the effort to meditate and practice Dharma. Then you will really be doing something good for yourself.

If you are not able to do Dharma practice and are instead fully distracted by mundane life, believing that obtaining material success is the best thing you can do for yourself, then, at the time of death, you will face the fact that all your material success has to be left behind, and you have not done much good for yourself at all. What is beneficial at the time of death and after death is the experience developed through meditation and Dharma practice.

If you understand this, you must learn to integrate daily life with your practice. Sometimes we practice the Dharma and meditation, but we still do not know the proper attitude to take. We think, "I want to practice the Dharma in order to experience success and well-being in this lifetime." But even though you practice, you do not experience any success or well-being. At that point you start to wonder, "Is the Dharma really working? Isn't it supposed to work?" But what you don't realize is that you have a great deal of karma to purify. Although the practice you are doing might purify this karma, it is not immediately apparent or visible. As a result, you may begin to doubt your Dharma practice, and might even give it up. But when you cultivate a seed, you have to wait to experience its fruit. When you experience its fruit, then you cultivate the seed again. You cannot experience all these things simultaneously. Likewise, we have to wait to purify our negative karma in order to experience positive karma.

Some people are fortunate and do experience the outcome of their practice fairly quickly, but this shows that their accumulation of negative karma was light. Because there was only a thin layer of negative karma, positive practice was able to eliminate it completely.

Another important point about integrating practice into daily life is that we must never underestimate the power of virtuous action. Sometimes, the amount of time we can dedicate to practice every day is quite minimal. We may feel that it is not benefiting us because the time spent is so little. However, if we do the practice properly, it could be of tremendous help. It is like a large tree. It started out as a tiny seed, but under the proper conditions—good environment, rich soil, water, light, and warmth—that small seed had the capacity to develop into something gigantic. But all the conditions had to be met. If the seed was just thrown onto sand, for example, it could not have grown into a tree. Someone might then conclude that there was something wrong with the seed, but there was nothing wrong with it. It was just planted in the wrong place.

Similarly, with regard to your practice, even if you are doing it for just a short time every day, if you concentrate on the practice, recognize that it benefits all sentient beings, and dedicate the merit to all of them without attachment to your own welfare, then you have cultivated the seed in the right way. In this way, a short period of regular practice has the capacity to develop into something vast and profound.

QUESTIONS & ANSWERS

STUDENT: I'd like to go back to the example you used to help us understand non-reality, where we take an object and break it down into different parts. I have a hard time understanding that. You take a table, and you divide it into different components and different components and different components, but in the end, you still have a collection of something. That is a different way of seeing it, but it is not a negation of its reality.

RINPOCHE: We experience ordinary perceptions as real, but they are only a relative truth. Relative truths seem to be very real, yet they are not completely true, which is why they are called relative truth and not absolute. It is a relative truth because due to the presence of karma, experiences seem real and perhaps cause pain. However, once you have eliminated karmic obscurations, these things do not exist. When you break everything down into say atoms or subatomic particles, then who is it that knows that these things exist? We would say that it is the mind that knows this. If you then look into the mind, the knower of the existence of the particles, and are asked where this mind is, you cannot find an entity that is this perceiver or mind. Something that does not exist cannot define whether something else exists or not.

STUDENT: I think I have intellectually understood the idea that everything is impermanent, and at the end everything will decompose into the elements or into its components again. As you explained, though, my mind is always distracted. I seem to forget this, and always go back to seeing everything as permanent, forgetting that I have to die sometime, and that I don't know when that will be. How can I remember this more consistently, and maintain mindfulness so that my awareness does not wander away so easily?

RINPOCHE: To develop authentic mindfulness is very difficult. That is true for everyone. There are two things which may help with this, though I cannot promise they will help in every case.

The first thing is simply to do shamata meditation. I do not mean that just sitting silently will produce good mindfulness. However, understanding shamata, getting some experience with it, and developing the qualities that come from it can be of help. Shamata literally means developing calm abiding of the mind. Cultivating this calm abiding has definitely helped people develop consistent mindfulness.

The other thing that can actually bring about mindfulness is experiencing something really painful and unpleasant. For example, say you are walking down the street and step into a hole and twist your ankle. The next time you walk by that place you are going to remember the hole and not step in it. Thus, the painful experience helped you to be mindful not to make the same mistake again. Or, perhaps you walk into a house, and the door frame is quite low and you bang your head. The next time you enter the house, you are going to duck. In a more extreme case, perhaps someone very dear to you dies. That sort of experience helps us realize that we, too, will die one day, which leads us to be really mindful of impermanence.

STUDENT: I'm wondering about wrath in the sense that in that case there is also a difference between appearance and reality.

RINPOCHE: As you say, in terms of appearance, anger and wrath are very similar, but internally there is a difference. Anger is associated with really wanting to hurt, harm, or destroy another person. Wrath may look the same externally, but the intention is very different. It is sometimes used in order to correct someone who has been misbehaving. For instance, you might use wrath if you have been gentle with someone but they fail to listen to or apply your advice. It seems like you are angry, but your intention is to help the person. That wrath is acceptable, because there is no malicious feeling involved.

At the same time, you must be very skillful when you use a wrathful approach. You must not use it repeatedly because if you do, the other person may take it seriously and feel that your intention is to harm them, and they will turn away from you in hurt and anger. You must also learn to show love to the person and help them understand your intention. Then the other person will realize that your wrathfulness is really an effort to help, not hurt. Behaving in a wrathful way with the absence of real anger is skillful means.

STUDENT: Can wrath be described as being like a role in a play or film, where the actor understands he is playing a role and not actually fulfilling the role in his consciousness? In other words, is it an act, a portrayal of anger in the name of altruism, where you are not agitated internally as you would be if you were angry? Or do you in fact get internally agitated?

RINPOCHE: It's really both. It's based on the spiritual development of the individual. If the individual is quite advanced spiritually, then the wrath is like acting. His or her mind is not touched by anger at all, and their altruism, their bodhicitta, is unshaken. As a result, that person can enact, physiologically so to speak, the appearance of anger. In the case of ordinary individuals—those not spiritually advanced—they can also show wrathfulness in order to correct another person, but sometimes their wrathfulness turns into anger. Although this anger is still not positive, it's not as negative as it would normally be because it has nothing to do with wanting to hurt or destroy someone. The anger which arises in this situation is due to wanting to correct the other person, and the intention was to help. It's all based on your level of spiritual development.

It's very interesting that someone could be very wrathful, but actually could be trying to be good and kind and act for your benefit. In other cases, someone could seem to be very kind and gentle, but internally be quite malicious and resentful. You can never really judge a person from external appearances. It's all based on internal attitude.

STUDENT: It seems, especially for beginners like me, that much of my accumulation of negative karma is due to reacting, especially when I react too quickly. Does that mean that one of the first areas we need to work on is to be less impulsive, such that we can take some time before reacting?

RINPOCHE: Yes. That's when the intellectual understanding of Buddhism, the practice of tonglen, and the development of loving-kindness and compassion become quite helpful. The view of Buddhism is that all the phenomena and experiences we have are not real, so you learn not to take difficult experiences so seriously. The practice aspect of sending and receiving helps you to develop love and compassion so that when you are faced with a situation, you are accustomed to maintaining an attitude of love and compassion. In this way, you are able to avoid being reactive.

Having an intellectual understanding of the view is not enough. If you have not previously developed sending and receiving in your meditation practice, you may not be able to practice it when difficult situations arise. You need to become accustomed to behaving in this manner; you need to combine the view with actual practice. Otherwise, you will simply react as you have in the past, with anger, jealousy, and so forth. This is why preparation is necessary, and the preparation comes from the practice.

STUDENT: Would you expand on the ultimate nature of phenomena?

RINPOCHE: The ultimate nature of phenomena is really quite a difficult concept to understand and explain. However, I can explain it by referring to the traditional teachings in the texts. Keep in mind that getting a conceptual explanation of this ultimate nature without some direct experience through meditation might not help very much.

Having said that, conceptually speaking, the ultimate nature of phenomena is discussed in terms of *shunyata* or emptiness. This does not mean the absence or the disappearance of all phenomena. Another incorrect understanding of emptiness is thinking that when the concreteness of phenomena—the feeling that it seems so solid and real—disappears, then emptiness or shunyata appears. This interpretation separates phenomena and emptiness from each other, and that is not the right approach either.

The correct concept of the ultimate nature of phenomena would be that phenomena—which means whatever we are experiencing—has no true essence. Phenomena appear to us just like an image in a mirror, or the arising of appearances in a dream. Reflections in a mirror and events in dreams have no essence, but at the moment we experience them they seem concrete and real. By developing the knowledge that all external phenomena are by nature without essence, we will get closer to understanding the ultimate nature.

Credits

All of the teachings in this book are edited versions of talks given by Ven. Khenpo Karthar Rinpoche between 1984-1993. It was originally published as a transcript entitled *Transforming Mental Afflictions*, under the supervision of Michael and Margaret Erlewine at Heart Center KTC in Big Rapids, Michigan. It was edited by Robert Walker.

Hearing, Contemplation, and Meditation—How to Attain the Fruition of Buddhist Practice, is based on a talk given April 25, 1986 at KTD Monastery, Woodstock, NY. It first appeared in *Densal Magazine*, Vol. VII, No. 3, under the title How to be a Darling of the World. Translated by Chöjor Radha. Transcriptionist unknown. Original edit by Andrea Price; further editing by Robert Walker.

Connecting With the Dharma is based on a talk given August 13, 1985 at KTD Monastery, Woodstock, NY. It first appeared in *Densal Magazine*, Vol. VI, No. 4, under the title Buddhism and the Mind. Translated by Ngödup Burkhar. Transcriptionist unknown. Original edit by Michelle Martin; further editing by Robert Walker.

The Essence of the Teachings of the Buddha seminar was given in November 1989 at KTD Monastery, Woodstock, NY. Translated by Chöjor Radha. Transcriptionist: Jeanette DeFries. Transcription checked by Tim Roark. Edited by Robert Walker in consultation with the translator.

Transforming Mental Afflictions seminar was given in November 1992 at Seattle KKSG. Translated by Lama Yeshe Gyamtso. Transcriptionist: Gwen Merrick. Transcription checked by Robert Walker and Ken Bacher. Edited by Ken Bacher and Robert Walker in consultation with the translator.

THE FOUR IMMEASURABLES seminar was given April 22-24, 1988 in Columbus, Ohio. Translated by Ngödup Burkhar. Transcriptionist: David Moore. Transcription checked by Jonathan Derr and Robert Walker. Edited by Robert Walker and Jonathan Derr in consultation with Chöjor Radha.

THE BODHISATTVA PATH seminar was given in June of 1984 at KTD Monastery, Woodstock, NY. Translated by Chöjor Radha. Transcriptionist: Tana Basham-Hobart. Transcription checked by Bill Williams and Robert Walker. Edited by Robert Walker and Bill Williams in consultation with the translator.

PREPARING TO TAKE THE BODHISATTVA VOW: THE SEVEN BRANCH OFFERINGS was given in August of 1985 at KTD Monastery, Woodstock, NY. Translated by Chöjor Radha. Transcriptionist: Peter Crockett. Transcription checked by Peter Crockett and Robert Walker. Edited by Robert Walker in consultation with the translator.

THE IMPORTANCE OF HAVING A SPIRITUAL FRIEND was given January 16, 1990 in Albuquerque, New Mexico. It first appeared in *Densal magazine,* Vol. XIII, No. 3 under the title The Importance of a Spiritual Friend. Transcriptionist: Unknown. Translated by Chöjor Radha. Checked and edited by Ken Bacher, with Robert Walker.

THE AUTHENTIC MASTER, THE AUTHENTIC STUDENT is based on a talk given in December of 1988 at KTD Monastery, Woodstock, NY. It was first published in *Densal magazine,* Vol. IX, No. 4. Translated by Chöjor Radha. Original editing by Sally Clay; further editing by Robert Walker.

THE FOUR FOUNDATIONS OF MINDFULNESS is a teaching given in September, 1993. Translated by Chöjor Radha. Transcribed by Karma Chonyi Zangmo (Pamela Holtum). Edited by Drolma Birney.